Advance Praise for
Looking to Write: Students Writing through the Visual Arts

This book will take your breath away. Read it many times. Read it through the eyes of a writing teacher, an art historian, a political activist, a guidance counselor, a reading specialist, an adolescent. With each reading, discover how Mary Ehrenworth is not simply determined to harness the power of the visual arts to strengthen student writing. No, Mary challenges her readers to make the world a better place. She asks us to take risks, to grapple with complex and difficult issues that force us to rethink what it means to be human. She inspires and instructs students and teachers to treat one another with respect, dignity, and love.

This book will provoke lively, controversial and significant conversations in classrooms as well as in staff rooms. Written with intimacy, passion and a wide-world of expertise, Mary asks her readers to put sexism, racism, homophobia, and violence on their front burners. She surrounds students with carefully selected and researched paintings, sculpture, and artifacts, matching those with genres that include poetry, narrative, short story, and myth. The text brims with intriguing art photographs, examples of Mary's own writing, teaching and storytelling, as well as student work samples. She provides practical and fresh supports for struggling or complacent students, including observations, storytelling, teacher modeling, partnerships, side-by side conversations, and templates to follow.

No doubt, teachers will lift quotations from this book, as each page is studded with big ideas. I found myself highlighting, scribbling in the margins, adding exclamation points, and drawing happy faces. Mary offers the kind of words that renew educators' commitment to their students, to their profession, to the arts, to literacy learning, and above all to peace on Earth and good will to all of humankind. Mary Ehrenworth's words, "To teach writing as a way to care for the world, and for each other, and to find things in the world to love, and things to hold onto," are now posted above my writing desk.

—*Shelley Harwayne*
Superintendent, New York City
Public Schools

Looking *to* Write

Looking *to* Write

**Students
Writing
Through the
Visual Arts**

Mary
Ehrenworth

HEINEMANN
Portsmouth, NH

Heinemann
A division of Reed Elsevier Inc.
361 Hanover Street
Portsmouth, NH 03801–3912
www.heinemann.com

Offices and agents throughout the world

The author and publisher wish to thank those who have generously given permission to reprint borrowed material:

El Guernica by Pablo Picasso. Artists Rights Society, New York, and Art Resource, New York. Copyright © 2003 Estate of Pablo Picasso/Artists Rights Society, New York. Image Copyright © John Bigelow Taylor/Art Resource, NY.

Portrait of Olga in an Armchair by Pablo Picasso. Artists Rights Society, New York, and Art Resource, New York. Copyright © 2003 Estate of Pablo Picasso/Artists Rights Society, New York. Image Copyright © Réunion de Musées Nationaux/ Art Resource, NY.

Woman in White by Pablo Picasso. The Metropolitan Museum of Art, Rogers Fund, 1951: acquired from the Museum of Modern Art, Lillie P. Bliss Collection. (53.140.4) Photograph © 1994 by The Metropolitan Museum of Art.

(continued on page viii)

Library of Congress Cataloging-in-Publication Data
Ehrenworth, Mary.
    Looking to write : students writing through the visual arts / Mary Ehrenworth.
        p. cm.
    Includes bibliographical references and index.
    ISBN 0-325-00463-3 (pbk. : alk. paper)
    1. Creative writing (Secondary education). 2. Art—Study and teaching
(Secondary). I. Title.

    LB1631.E47 2003
    808'.042'0712—dc21   2003009546

Editor: Kate Montgomery
Production: Lynne Reed
Cover design: Lisa Fowler
Compositor: Drawing Board Studios/Valerie Levy
Manufacturing: Steve Bernier

Printed in the United States of America on acid-free paper
07 06 05 VP 2 3 4 5

To
Andy and Jackson Ehrenworth
and
Kay and Paul Lohnes

Foreword

Those who teach with the hope of releasing the young from silence or from an unthinking compliance with the conventions of their world cannot but be lured into dialogue by this book. I have in mind a dialogue with this marvelously perceptive writer. Concerned for ways of knowing, seeing, and, yes, feeling, she entices us to ponder the possibility of enabling diverse young people to make their imprints on the world.

She knows that one's becoming ("becoming different," as Dewey used to say) cannot happen without a context, a fabric of suggestive sights and sounds, an environment that is always somehow incomplete, calling on all who attend to reach beyond. Most significantly, the author begins with the events of September 11, 2001: the devastation of neighborhoods; the response of the children and their teachers; the desperate need for hope, for shared understanding, for some means of confronting a sudden consciousness of vulnerability—indeed, of the human condition.

We are made aware again of the need to find a means of expression not only for dread but for longing and empathy. There was a void most of us remember; and Mary Ehrenworth opens a range of perspectives on what teachers can do—in collaboration with their students—to fill that void. This book expands and deepens our own awareness of both aesthetic and pedagogic possibility by providing us with instance after instance of young people being empowered to see by looking at and attending to a variety of paintings and sculptures—those studding our and other traditions like points of light, artworks the author herself obviously knows and loves. Her descriptions, the ways in which she offers paintings to the young for their interpretations, give her readers a sense of the passion that infuses this particular teacher's seeing and feeling and knowing. We grasp the ways in which such capacities (intelligences, if we prefer) create new orders, new openings as they come together. The inclusion of children's writing, inspired by the paintings and sculptures, may well be unforgettable. This preface writer is made eager to bring other young ones to pay heed to the Picassos, the Matisses, the Jacob Lawrences, the Mary Cassatts. What would they say? How would they see? Would any of them notice what Picasso did in imaging Olga early and late? Would they notice a missing button on a Civil War soldier's uniform—and try to put down on paper their view of what Winslow Homer had in mind?

Looking *to* Write

There must be work that we can do in schools as an antidote to this kind of reiteration of hostile isolationism and antipathy to others. There have to be ways to invoke sentiments of sympathy, of recognition of common interests, of consciousness of experiences that traverse national borders and transcend individual histories. There have to be ways for teachers to invent what Maxine Greene calls "the kinds of situations where individuals come together in such a way that each one feels a responsibility for naming the humane and the desirable and moving together to attain them" (2000a, 274).

When I think about Maxine's words, I want to participate in this move toward attaining the humane. For me, that has meant inventing meaningful ways to engage children with the visual arts in the teaching of writing. For it is the arts that illuminate the human condition. It is through the arts that we can most easily come together in ways that cultivate sympathetic understanding. "Sympathy," says Dewey, "as a desirable quality is more than mere feeling; it is a cultivated imagination for what men have in common and a rebellion at whatever unnecessarily divides them" (1916/1944, 121). Incorporating the arts in our teaching helps us actively teach and practice sympathetic understanding. Incorporating the arts in the teaching of writing helps us teach students expressive ways to communicate this understanding.

I started teaching as an aspiring art historian, and the first seven years I taught, I spent every single day looking at paintings and sculptures with children and adults. We pondered the nature of the cave paintings of Altamira; we gloried in exhibitions like the Byzantium exhibition at the Metropolitan Museum and the Vermeer exhibition at the National Gallery; we knew where paintings and sculptures were in the city, and which ones would be traveling, and how we could get to see them. When I moved into the public schools to teach reading and writing, I thought it meant abandoning this intimate teaching relationship with the visual arts. Despite the privilege of reading and writing with children, I still felt a kind of underlying sadness.

The ideas of two women helped me name and rebel at this loss. Reading Maxine Greene, I came to realize that the gradual disappearance of the arts from public schooling was of national concern and that there were people who cared about this decline and were working against it. Moreover, Maxine makes clear that there is work to do in keeping the arts in schooling and that there is work to do in engaging the arts in meaningful ways in the curriculum. She asserts that

> informed engagements with the several arts is the most likely mode of releasing our students' (or any person's) imaginative capacity and giving it play. However, this will not, cannot, happen automatically or "naturally." . . . Aesthetic experiences require conscious participation in a work, a going out of energy, an ability to notice what is there to be noticed. (1995, 125)

I wanted to "notice what there is to be noticed" with children. I wanted to see what it means to try to orchestrate aesthetic experiences in the classroom. A com-

FIGURE I–1   The Rocky Mountains, Lander's Peak,
Bierstadt (detail)

mon experience for teachers and graduate students, though, is that we read the ideas of philosophers, we come to care about these ideas, but we still need to articulate what these philosophical endeavors will mean in our teaching. Just as we do daily lesson plans to envision how our classroom will look and what the children will be doing, we have to examine the curriculum and think about how to weave our educational concerns into it. For me, that meant thinking about encounters with the visual arts as potentially generative in the teaching of writing. I looked at things children had written in response to the visual arts, entries such as the following one by third grader Mary. Mary wrote this notebook entry in a museum with my after-school group, where we looked at Bierstadt's 1863 grand, panoramic painting of the Shoshone Indians in their Rocky Mountain retreat (see Figure I–1).

Mary looked, and she wrote:

> The Shoshone Indians are in the mountains in a place where the mountains meet the sky and the hills meet the mountains and the forest meets the hills. The snow comes down from the mountains and makes waterfalls and it is where the waterfall meets the forest that the Shoshone Indians are. The Shoshone women and the Shoshone children. The Shoshone men. The Shoshone boys. The Shoshone horses. The Shoshone wear brown clothes the color of the mountains. Their horses are brown, and so are their houses. If you didn't look hard you would miss them
> I wonder if they want to be missed.

There is something powerful in the way children mentor themselves to art the same way they might mentor themselves to a piece of literature. Bierstadt's painting is sweeping in its vision and acute in its detail. It suggests that the Shoshone live in harmony with the natural world. It somehow implies the beauty but also the precarious state of their retreat. Mary does these same things in her writing. Implicit in her writing is the sense of mountains and hills and forests and Shoshone existing together. And yet within this natural harmony, Mary notices that there are smaller groupings. The women and the children. The boys, who are separate from this group. The men. Mary makes these groups individual in her description and she still preserves a sense of their interdependence with each other and the landscape.

I didn't teach Mary to write these things. I taught her to look closely, and in her looking, she found things to write about and ways to write them that reflected her aesthetic interaction with this painting. And I learned to look closely at her writing in the same ways that I wanted her to look closely at the painting. I saw that Mary's writing evokes relationships and emotional landscapes just as the painting does. When I began working more formally as a writing teacher, I wanted to continue this kind of work and to think about what, in fact, we could do in our teaching to make these aesthetic experiences even more effective in the teaching of writing.

Of course, sometimes we run into obstacles in the form of dogmatism. I have been fortunate indeed in having Shelley Harwayne, superintendent of what has been New York City Community School District Two and is now part of Re-

FIGURE I–2   *Olga in armchair* (detail), Carrie's drawing

Olga

On the canvas
my hair is smooth and long,
my arms white
and my lips red.
How long will
Picasso think I'm beautiful?

gion Nine, as an instructional leader in the teaching of reading and writing. At a workshop early in my career as a literacy staff developer, Shelley said two things. She referred to Don Murray's idea that there is no one way to teach writing (1968) as a watershed. And she said that she hoped that teachers would always share their great passions with children, that they would show children and other teachers what it was like to care deeply about a subject and to want others to care. Shelley gave me the confidence to say that I care about engaging children with the visual arts, and that I believe that things happen in children's writing when they write through the arts that do not, perhaps, happen through other ways of teaching writing. It can be an aesthetic experience, a way to engage the imagination in peculiarly empathetic ways.

We see this potential for empathy, for instance, when thirteen-year-old Carrie looks at two of Picasso's paintings of Olga (see Figure I–2 and I–3 for Carrie's interpretations of these paintings), and she writes these poems.

Carrie is thirteen years old. She doesn't know what it feels like to be Olga, to leave the Ballet Russe to marry Picasso, to have him take up a younger woman, a

FIGURE I–3   *Seated Bather* (detail), Carrie's drawing

Olga

When did I become a monster?
Jagged bones,
an insect's head
You gave me a skeleton
but no heart.
You have devoured me.

girl really, or to be portrayed on the canvas as a monster by Picasso. But clearly she can imagine it. Carrie's poems let us see two things happening that matter for teaching and for the teaching of writing. The first is that Carrie is able to imagine what it feels like to be Olga because she has an aesthetic experience with these paintings. Not only does she look closely at the paintings, but she participates in them. *You have devoured me.* Art theorist John Berger says that "seeing comes before words. The child looks and recognizes before it can speak" (1977, 7). We teach children the ways of written language. The ways of knowing through looking are more tacit.

And when Carrie makes meaning, she creates another aesthetic object, which is also significant. I do think that we have to pay close attention to the ways children's writing operates aesthetically. Carrie's poems give us yet another perspective, another possible way to envision the experience of fear and loss marked by Olga's transformation on the canvas. Carrie's poems *feel* true. She might or might not know what love feels like, or what it means to be abandoned, or what it feels like to see your body change in monstrous ways. But in whatever way she knows these things, through her interaction with the paintings and with poetry, Carrie finds a way to let us know them. Maxine Greene (2000b, 298) writes that "the notion of multiple and provisional perspectives fuses with a vision of spaces that are not closed in, that are open on all sides to the unexpected and the possible . . . who comes closer to the truth—the poet or the political theorist?" Carrie's poetry demonstrates the possibility that children are able to excavate many perspectives and many ways of knowing. Engaging them with the arts can lead to both the unexpected and the possible in their writing.

There is also a way that engaging with painting and sculpture helps us teach children to be careful observers. It feels like this world would be a better place if we just listened more and looked more closely. Consider fourteen-year-old Julia,

FIGURE I–4   *Head of an Oba* (detail)

who looks at a sculpture from Benin, an altar head of the *Oba*, the king (see Figure I–4). She knows that altar heads like this reflected individual obas and were sacred objects, believed to give present obas the power to communicate with their ancestors. She knows this information through historical inquiry. But in looking closely, Julia comes to know the nature of the Oba in a way she would not through historical research alone. As Julia looks, she takes some notes and then she freewrites (Rief 1992). In her notes she jots down:

> over-life size maybe? Smooth skin but row of scars on the forehead. The scars bulge—symmetrical, three on either side. Long hair braided into tiny sidelocks. Eyes that stare straight ahead—outlined and exaggerated. Nose perfectly straight and right exactly over the mouth. Mouth is kind of pursed and held in that position by the necklaces. There are sixty ? necklaces and they cover the neck entirely and keep the chin up and the head held in one position. The hair comes exactly to the bottom of the necklaces. There is a cap with some kind of decoration on top, also braided, with symmetrical designs.

Julia has noticed a lot of detail simply by staying with it, by "noticing what there is to be noticed." It is how this noticing leads to imaginative leaps, however, that seems significant. Freewriting just below these jottings, Julia writes:

> If I were Oba, would I have the courage to have someone cut into my face with a knife? When the point sliced into my skin would it hurt? Would it be exhilarating? Or would I want to run and hide in my mother's arms? Could I stay unmoving, for the six times the knife came close?
>
> When I put on the cap, would I feel like a king? Would I feel the coral bead necklaces holding up my chin and know that I would never see the ground again—and that would let me know that I was king? Would I look at the altar heads and think—that will be me some day? I will be a spirit. Or would I look at my hands and wonder how this will all happen? Will I wonder how this boy, this boy who is me, this me who is a boy, is going to become all these things?

When Julia looks closely, she begins to question not only what she sees but what she feels about what she sees, and even what it might mean to be the Oba seeing and feeling. Julia is responding aesthetically to the expressiveness implicit in some sculptures. Eisner looks at how artists work to reveal expressive qualities, and he asks:

> Why have artists been interested in such tasks? Why should such efforts occupy a central place in the history of the arts? At least a part of the reason is because much of what is most important in human experience is not what is apparent, but, instead, what is felt about what is apparent. Things are not always what they appear to be on the surface. They need to be seen in terms of the kind of emotional life they that they generate." (1994, 53)

What we see in Julia's writing is a child responding to the emotional life generated by this object. We see Julia trying to write this felt emotional life into existence. Julia continues this work when she writes a short story about a boy who does not know how to pray becoming Oba. Her story becomes more of an exploration of inner feelings than a description of outer details. The generative work of this writing, however, began with Julia's looking closely, which is part of her aesthetic experience with this object.

Maxine Greene (1995) returns often to the question, What *is* an aesthetic experience? If we focus on the notion of what makes an experience aesthetic, I think that it is the quality of actively engaging with an object or text and making meaning through that participatory engagement. But there is still the question of What is experience, and which experiences are educative? Dewey laments that "ordinary experience is often infected with apathy, lassitude, and stereotype. We get neither the impact of quality through sense nor the meaning of things through thought" (1934/1980, 260). When we ask children to write through their engagement with the visual arts, we ask them both to make sense of what they see and to make meaning on the page. In this way we orchestrate an experience for the children that has aesthetic potential. Dewey describes this kind of experience as one that

> signifies active and alert commerce with the world; at its height it signifies complete interpenetration of the self and the world of objects and events. . . . Because experience is the fulfillment of an organism in its struggles and achievements in a world of things, it is art in germ. Even in its rudimentary forms, it contains the promise of that delightful perception which is esthetic experience. (1934/1980, 19)

Delightful perception. That should be an aim in teaching and learning. It feels like the language of schooling has changed so much, that the very way we describe education has become the language of factories, of standardization and accountability. Education needs to be an art, not an industry.

nonchalant about things I never dreamed of" (McCracken 2002, 193). Stories make multiple existences seem possible. And again, the sculptures help in this work because they make the narrative one of beauty. And so the next poem I share with the students is a two-voice poem that tells how the flower hyacinth grows from Apollo's love for the boy of that name, just as the constellation Orion grows from the desire between Orion and Artemis. In the narrative gap left in Ovid's telling, I tell them how this could have happened, how perhaps these two loves were complicated by another love, that of the brother for the sister. I am deliberately complicating notions of love and desire that have come to seem unilateral.

In my poem, Apollo, in jealousy that human Orion desires his sister, leads Artemis to unknowingly slay Orion. In return, Artemis engineers the slaughter of Hyacinth, the boy whom Apollo loves. In two-voice poems, two readers are necessary, and they read consecutively going down the page, except where the lines are the same, when they read at the same time and their voices overlap.

Artemis	*Apollo*
The Death of Orion	The Death of Hyacinth
I saw him first in the woods	**I saw him first in the** training grounds
He was hunting	**He was** wrestling
His hair was long and brown tied back with a leather thong	**His hair was** short and fair pushed off his forehead with a band
His skin was rough and sunburnt	**His skin was** smooth and golden
I watched him for nights	**I watched him** for days

Until I knew	**Until I knew**
the sounds he made while sleeping	the way he moved
While he slept I	**While he slept I**
touched his lashes with my tongue	
	brushed my fingers over his chest
One night he awakened	**One night he awakened**
and pulled me down beside him	
	and stood swiftly over me
and looked at me with love	**and looked at me with love**
I loved to touch the bones of his hips	
and the skin of **his pelvis**	. . . . **his pelvis**,
	his hands, the back of his neck
	where the hair curled
When	
	Why
did you decide to take him from me?	**did you decide to take him from me?**
	We were training on the fields
We were hunting in the woods	
	Playing with the discus
with the bow	
It was a contest	**It was a contest**
I hadn't yet decided if	
	I had decided that
I would let him win	**I would let him win**
He turned to look at me	
	He sparkled as he ran
His face full	**His face full**
of laughter	
	of love
But you guided	**But you guided**
my arrow	
	my discus

From the heat of your spirit

                From the coldness of your heart

It entered through his side
   and quivered in his lung

                It struck in the forehead and the
                   blood poured down

He cried **my name**
   as he died

          . . . . **my name** was on his lips
          as he died

I couldn't die

                I wanted to die

I made him
                I made him
                   a flower

   a belt of stars

   I wish **I could hate you**
                . . . . **I could hate you**

This is what I mean by trying to bring theoretical concerns into the classroom by writing for the children. The children know that the work of our myths is to explain how something came to be. So they are with me from the start in understanding that I will explain the existence of the stars that make up the constellation Orion and the flower that we call the hyacinth. They have followed me with my first poem into understanding the notion of desire in the relationship between Apollo and Artemis. Now they hear how Apollo loves the boy Hyacinth, and it is not so surprising that the pain and joy of this love feel akin to those of other loves. And Greek sculptures helps make it clear that Hyacinth is, indeed, a boy. It keeps the students from resisting this knowledge, from thinking of him as a girl, which is what many of them want to do. It also lets them know that this story has been told before, and that if they haven't heard stories of this kind of love, then it is simply because they haven't looked for them.

I think we can expect that through storytelling, children will follow us onto ground that otherwise might seem dangerous. And that can be fertile ground for them as writers. Look at what Elai, an eighth grader, does in his myth. Describing the sculpture *Dying Gaul* as a fallen warrior who went into battle with his lover, Elai writes:

> Alexander stood over Diomedes's body
> and looked at it with love and horror.
> Where was the wound?
> And then he saw the blood seeping from beneath the armor.
> A javelin must have pierced him
> under the arm where the leather parted.
> They taught the Gauls to look for the place.

He stood over the body
and decided that he would not leave this spot.
And he raised his sword calmly
to face the enemy rushing toward him.
He brought ten of them with him into the dark

And since that day
the Greeks save the Sacred Band, the legion of warrior-lovers
for their most desperate defenses
not because they are the most skilled warriors
but because they know the meaning of honor.

Elai accomplishes many things here in his writing. He is constructing homosexuality as an honorable form of masculinity. He is looking closely at the sculpture and imagining narrative possibility from it. He is writing in clear, spare, beautiful language. And I think some of this work arises from two ways that Elai interacts with me. Much of my teaching of writing occurs in side-by-side conversations with students, where I try to name what they are doing in their writing and show them ways that they could continue this work, or ways that might make the work they have begun more clear or more beautiful. And so I see, and tell Elai that I see, him trying to provoke an aesthetic response to the notion of homosexuality by making something that is a thing of beauty. But the other way that Elai interacts with me is that his writing is in a conversation with my writing. Elai's story is intermingled with my stories and they are both affected by and will affect our classroom environment. Donald Graves tells us that "there is something sacred about a story. When we attend to children's stories, we establish probably the best foundation for their own future as learners. We therefore have to ask ourselves if stories are an essential element in our curriculum" (2002, 17).

Sometimes it is in response to stories they hear and images they see that adolescents can envision identities and possibilities that otherwise seem impossible. Kieran Egan claims that this coming to know is, in fact, the process of education, that "it is a process that awakens individuals to a kind of thought that enables them to imagine conditions other than those that exist or that have existed" (1992, 46). But I don't think this work happens unless we plan toward it and unless we risk—unless we are part of this process of locating self. Pinar asks us to think of curriculum in terms of forms of "indirect discourse" that would unsettle one's students, quietly institute a revolution in the self, and thereby unsettle extant social relations" (2001, 24). Of course, this work seems to matter only if we believe that there is a need to improve the extant social relations at work in the world and a need to revolutionize self, in part through writing and through our work.

I do believe this. I believe that there is work to do in making this world a better place. I believe there are ways to consider how to be a part of this work in my teaching. And I believe that in the teaching of writing especially, we can help children expand their ways of knowing themselves and the world. Shelley Harwayne says that "in our writing workshops, we must look through the lens of childhood" and we must be careful to "let children be children" (2001, xvi). She reminds me that if we take up theoretical concerns and issues of social justice in our classrooms, it will not be meaningful unless we maintain work that is appropriate for children. It feels appropriate for children to look at visual art and to write. It feels effective. And it feels meaningful. It is a way to value the presence of the arts in the world, it is a way to orchestrate aesthetic experiences in schooling, and it is a way to expand children's ways of knowing and ways of writing.

REFERENCES

Berger, J. 1977. *Ways of Seeing*. London: Penguin.

Davies, B. 1989. *Frogs and Snails and Feminist Tales: Preschool Children and Gender*. Sydney: Allen and Unwin.

Dewey, J. 1916/1944. *Democracy and Education: An Introduction to the Philosophy of Education*. New York: Free Press.

———. 1934/1980. *Art as experience*. New York: Perigee.

Egan, K. 1992. *Imagination in Teaching and Learning: The Middle School Years*. Chicago: University of Chicago Press.

Eisner, E. 1994. *Cognition and Curriculum Reconsidered*. 2d ed. New York: Teachers College Press.

Graves, D. 2002. *Testing Is Not Teaching: What Should Count in Education*. Portsmouth, NH: Heinemann.

Greene, M. 1995. *Releasing the Imagination: Essays on Education, the Arts, and Social Change*. San Francisco: Jossey-Bass.

———. 2000a. "Imagining Futures: The Public School and Possibility." *Journal of Curriculum Studies* 32: 267–80.

———. 2000b "Lived Spaces, Shared Spaces, Public Spaces." In *Construction Sites: Excavating Race, Class, and Gender Among Urban Youth*, ed. M. Fine and L. Weiss, 293–304. New York: Teachers College Press.

Harwayne, S. 2001. *Writing Through Childhood: Rethinking Process and Product*. Portsmouth, NH: Heinemann.

Lesko, N. 2001. *Act Your Age: A Cultural Construction of Adolescence*. New York: Routledge Falmer.

McCracken, E. 2002. *Niagara Falls All Over Again*. New York: Delta.

Munsch, R. 1980/2002. *The Paper Bag Princess*. New York: Annick.

Murray, D. 1968. *A Writer Teaches Writing*. Portsmouth, NH: Heinemann.

Pinar, W. F. 1998. "Understanding Curriculum as Gender Text: Notes on Reproduction, Resistance, and Male-Male Relations." In *Queer Theory and Education*, ed. W. F. Pinar, 221–43. Mahwah, NJ: Lawrence Erlbaum.

———. 2001. *The Gender of Racial Politics and Violence in America*. New York: Peter Lang.

Rief, L. 1992. *Seeking Diversity*. Portsmouth, NH: Heinemann.

Romano, T. 1995. *Writing with Passion*. Portsmouth, NH: Heinemann.

———. 1999. *Blending Genres, Altering Styles*. Portsmouth, NH: Heinemann.

FIGURE 1–1   Guernica, Picasso

If Picasso Were Here, on September 11
(a poem inspired by *Guernica*, 1937)

If Picasso were here,
would he put the planes in his painting?
Pushing into the buildings like play-dough,
so silent on the television,
silent as the buildings falling
like tinker-toys or Lego blocks on those tiny screens.
But we felt them like an earthquake under us.
The school rocked
and the air turned gray
and we didn't know which way to run.

If Picasso were here,
would he put the firemen in,
holding up their lights
like moonbeams in the dark hallways?
Like the light in his painting,
that light bulb blazing with hope,
with truth and courage in a darkened world.

Would he paint the people jumping
from the high windows?
Or the people stepping over them?
Or the people on fire?
Or would he just show the city watching
and the children crying,
and that would be enough?

And does that light keep burning
even though they lost that Civil War in Spain,
the one he painted the painting about,
and we are, (we think), dropping bombs right now,
someplace in Afghanistan?
And if it is burning, can we see it?
Because we don't feel safe anymore
and we need someone to paint that light.

Many of us in schools turned to the arts both to express and to interpret the experiences of September 11. For me, the aftermath of September 11 has become a crucible for showing how a relationship with the arts helps students imagine connections between our experiences and those of others. We wrote ourselves into and out of paintings. We imagined our story in the shadow of other stories. We searched for visual and poetic imagery with which to explain the world and our place in it. We asked: How do artists and poets respond to calamity? That fall it seemed especially important to demonstrate to children alternative possibilities to the narratives of vengeance that arose so quickly in the media.

Television visualized that day for every American. The planes, the fires, the grief and shock. But television didn't move us forward. It didn't help the children or the teachers. Television seemed to keep us in that day. The buildings fell and fell. The schools evacuated, the children and teachers found their ways to safety. But we went back, right away, even though the televisions didn't show that. The air was full of smoke, a gray haze that hurt your throat bitterly, that burned the eyes and smelled of horrid things. And amidst the master narratives of resurgence that emerged so very quickly, this experience was somehow unspeakable. One school where I was teaching poetry was surrounded by militia and police. There were machine guns. There were bomb scares. The school had only two cell phones, and they worked only intermittently. The children would be riding the subway to school and suddenly the subway might stop and all passengers would be forced off at a strange station. Sometimes alone, the children would be unable to walk toward the school because the streets were cordoned off. There were anthrax scares. There was sudden homelessness and sudden poverty. It was such an unchildlike environment. It was very frightening for a very long time.

Maxine Greene writes that "the arts are on the margins of most of our lives, the margin being the place for those feelings and intuitions that daily life doesn't have a place for and mostly seems to suppress" (2000, 293). We felt, then, as if we lived and worked in the margins. We needed to learn there also. We needed to illumine those margins to see if we could express the anxieties and longings that were suppressed in the daily work of breathing the air downtown, of making ourselves go down into the subway, of looking through the air where the buildings had been.

Writing poetry gave us purpose. Looking at paintings gave vision to that purpose. I particularly looked with children downtown at Picasso's *El Guernica*, a painting of another bombing, another people who lost control of their own story line (see Figure 1–1, p. 18). Following Figure 1–1 is the poem that some sixth-grade students and I wrote together in a classroom downtown, smelling through our windows the fires still burning six weeks later, feeling the grit sharp in our eyes, and with a reproduction of Picasso's *El Guernica* in front of us.

Poetry as a Means for Children to Interpret and Reconstruct Experience

These middle school children, some of them relocated from their homes, some without electricity or water or phones, as they were to remain for weeks and even months to come, were not just shocked, but *displaced* by the violence that

FIGURE 1–2   Guernica, Picasso (detail)

had unfolded around them. They wrote, "If Picasso were here," words that express such a sense of the precarious, such longing for transformation. Poetry and painting became sites for the children where they could place that nexus of fear and longing and desire, where they could imagine some experience of transcendence. Picasso *is* here when the children write him into their poem. It is an inextricable tangle of artist, painting, and child. Looking at Picasso's painting helped us think about how painters, poets, and dancers express loss, and suffering, and fear, and the darkness of destruction as well as the light of hope. It helped us see that there are many ways to feel a sense of community, many ways to express outrage that do not betoken the death of another. Developing a relationship with this one painting helped us write and it helped us be in the world.

Interactive Looking and Writing: Making the Children's Words into Poetry

The way we came to write the poem was to first look at the painting for a long time. We looked at the figures twisted in the darkness. We looked at the way the human bodies were distorted in pain, so that everything that was beautiful became horrible. We looked at the recumbent male figure who was dismembered and killed, but still holds a broken sword in his closed fist in an expression of defiance. We looked at the mother cradling her dead child in her arms beneath the open window, her mouth spiky in grief and loss, the infant's head hanging lifeless (see Figure 1–2). We looked at the woman throwing up her arms beneath the flames in the darkened hallway, and at the woman whose leg seems to be injured; she drags it as if it were a great useless weight. And we looked at the light that spread over all the figures from the light bulb overhead and from the lantern thrust into the darkness.

Students can make great empathetic leaps as they look sometimes, if they understand the experiences in which the images are grounded. Then they can see how the artist interprets and expresses these experiences, and they can imagine how they, too, might take up this aesthetic work. I shared with the students how Picasso created *Guernica* in response to the deaths of the civilian population of the Basque town of Guernica. I told them how in the Spanish Civil War, in the shadow of the greater war to come, Guernica had been deliberately bombed by the Fascists as a way to test the notion of blitzkrieg, or total warfare, as a method for annihilating the spirit of the people and forcing them to submit. For the anti-Fascists, the painting existed as a beacon of hope and resistance, a means of depicting personal and national suffering and calling upon an international audience to come to their assistance.

The children listened carefully. This long-ago event did not seem so far away, with the painting in front of us and the smoke at the windows. I asked the children to consider how Picasso's painting seemed to relate to their experiences of September 11. As we pondered the light in the painting, many students talked about the light shed by firefighters who stayed inside the stairways of the World Trade Center, a light that allowed thousands to escape to safety. Somehow that light has come to mean something important to us in the city, as Picasso's bright light seems to light up more than a scene of human fear. It seems to suggest the possibility of human endeavor, and hope, and also the importance of bearing witness. As they thought, the children wrote or called out phrases, and we put them up on chart paper as an interactive writing exercise. Then I worked with them to relate their ideas back to what they saw in the painting, to repeat some phrases such as their first one, and then to work the poem into stanzas. And thus together, we made their phrases into the poem. Larry Fagin (2000) has a helpful description of how to work this way with children so that they can see their words as poetry. This kind of interactive looking and writing experience seems to really help young writers envision what the work of writing poetry can look like.

Poetry and Painting as Sustaining Forces for Children

Eisner (1994, 23) asks: "What kinds of meanings are accessible through the visual world?" In their interaction with this painting, the students engaged with a present calamity, they interrupted a narrative of vengeance that was coming to seem universal, and they related their own experiences to the imagined experiences of others through engaging with the art forms of painting and poetry. When we forge a relationship with the arts, we create the possibility of solace and strength and continued creativity. As Maxine Greene states so simply, "Artists know about spaces opening in the imagination, even as they understand what it means to be situated in the world" (2000, 293). It may be, in this modern world, that it is the arts that will carry us through times of great trouble, that will illuminate our condition in times to come. Of the many welcome and unwelcome lessons of September 11, one is that we must do everything in our power to strengthen our students' interaction with the arts, to see in them the possibility of creative and sustaining force. And we can start with something as simple as looking at paintings and looking to write.

Why Poetry, Why Painting?

We will not always be writing in the shadow of such a story as September 11. And yet students are often part of complicated story lines and are capable of immense empathy with imagined experience. We need to find ways to develop this empathy *and* the forms to communicate it. And there is simply no doubt that it is poetry, of all the writing of the world, that most lucidly articulates the human condition. It is in poetry that we sing our songs of praise and delight and sorrow and anger. As Maya Angelou writes:

> oh Black known and unknown poets, how often have your auctioned pains sustained us? Who will compute the lonely nights made less lonely by your songs or the empty pots made less tragic by your tales? . . . it may be enough, however, to have it said that we survive in exact relationship to the dedication of our poets. (1969/1993, 184)

Surely poetry is the solace and joy of the world. And so this workshop aims to put poetry in the hands of children and to affirm the worldly significance of poets and artists.

Painting can be a vehicle for developing empathetic engagement. It is a way into writing poetry, and it is also important in its own right. And so the aims of this workshop are threefold: to immerse the students in painting and portraiture, to absorb poetry, and to write poetry. The workshop I describe now, a poetry workshop inspired by Picasso's images of women, follows this structure: we will look at a group of paintings; we will become intimate with the imagery; we will articulate the visual language of the images; and we will forge links between visual and poetic language. This is how we will come to write. I like to conduct this workshop at the beginning of the year. It helps establish the classroom as a place involved with the arts in serious and constructive ways. The work of looking closely at imagery and deliberating word choice sharpens the students' analytical skills and enriches the language of the classroom. The time spent intimately engaged with the paintings becomes a way of looking and being in the world.

I use the term *workshop* in its more artistic sense, as in when we are working together in a studio. I do ask the students to engage with the paintings in order to write. I am orchestrating certain genre choices some of the time. Partly I use the term simply because this occupies the space of writing workshop in the curriculum. Also I expect the students to carry with them the ideas about autonomy over their process that they learn so well in writing workshop, as Lucy Calkins (1996) describes it. I think of the work sometimes as a genre study and sometimes as a craft study, and often this work is part of a larger study, for instance, a poetry unit where the students are reading and writing poetry in many ways. But there is no doubt that my purpose is twofold. One of those purposes is to find effective ways to initiate writing. The second is to engage students in a relationship with the arts.

Underlying this workshop is the belief that there is a way in which the visual arts express meaning that is different from other modes of representation. "Each form of representation," writes Eisner, "has a special contribution to make to the human experience" (1994, 19). An art object not only portrays an event or a figure but reveals how the artist *felt* about that subject. Moreover, that sense of the felt is peculiarly accessible to the young, who sometimes know more than they can say, who sometimes feel more than they may write. Eisner adds that education "ought to enable the young to learn how to access the meanings that have been created through . . . forms of representation . . . without the ability to 'read' the special and unique meanings that different forms of representation make possible, their content will remain for them an untappable resource, an enigma that they cannot solve" (1994, 19). I want, in this workshop, for us to devise access— access to the painted image, access to the written word, and access to all the insight of experience and expression that that access brings with it.

Of all those described in this book, this workshop particularly helps us consider the lifelong learning of students and hopes above all else to establish students in an intimate relationship with the arts. The arts, most especially the fine arts and poetry, have been too often reserved in schooling for a portion of the population that is considered to have merited access to it. This access seems to be merited by a sense of intellectual achievement—that is, these students have mastered the more urgent, functional forms of communication, and they may now be indulged with the teaching of artistic forms. But teaching poetry helps us teach writing that is lucid, and purposeful, and powerful.

"The language of poetry is a language of inquiry" writes poet Lyn Hejinian (2000, 3). More than any other written genre, poetry attempts to express the most through the least, to achieve the greatest clarity with the most rigorous discipline. Poetry is about profound investigation. And there is a reason that I link poetry with painting in this workshop: I think poetry and painting each have the ability to pick us up and move us to another place. They are among the most transformative modes of communication. They demonstrate what makes us human. Dewey asserts that art "strikes below the barriers that separate human beings from each other . . . art renders men [and women] aware of their union with one another in origin and destiny" (1934/1980, 272). I think of this workshop as a means of seeking out that union, of transcending barriers of age and experience, of finding ways to come together to cross the barricades that separate us.

Why Picasso?

The decision to look at Picasso's portraits of women for this poetry workshop reflects several interests. One is simply practical: paintings and drawings are much easier to reproduce and use in the classroom than are, for example, sculptures, artifacts, or objects. Another is that Picasso made so *many* images of women. It is relatively easy to go to the library, or access a museum or commercial website, or visit a bookstore, and come upon images of Picasso's women. And when we come upon these images, we come upon a conversation waiting to happen. There is a unifying focus—namely, the women—that gives us a place to start a conversation. There is terrific variety to stimulate comparison and interpretation. And there is a way to contain that conversation by focusing only on the women.

Children move forward quickly in developing understanding if we create some context for their initial looking through conversation. That is also why I like Picasso and Picasso's women. Picasso's biography is vivid and we don't have to (and never could) know it all in order to make provocative suggestions. His imagery is strong and clear. It is easy to compare the ways Picasso chooses to portray women, or at least it is easy to start that conversation. And that conversation models the kinds of conversation about choice, about communication, about expression, that we hope our students will have about writing and that we hope they will have beyond the doors of the classroom.

Four portraits of women who were intimately linked in one period of Picasso's life are reproduced on pages 28 and 29. I don't think you need to know more about these images than I am going to say here, which is what I say to my elementary and secondary students. I have included some more biographical information on Picasso in the Appendix, on pages 140–43. However, you do not need to be an expert on Picasso in order to orchestrate this workshop, and you do not need to be an art historian to explore the arts! It is inquiry that shapes the pedagogy of this workshop, not art history expertise.

If you want access to more images than those reproduced here, there are many books and cards available of Picasso's portraits. One of the most inclusive is the catalog *Picasso and Portraiture* (Rubin), from the 1996 exhibition at the Museum of Modern Art in New York. I often borrow several Picasso books from the library for this workshop, and I buy Picasso postcards whenever I am in museums or card shops. Some teachers I work with also purchase inexpensive posters from *www.art.com* so that the classroom can be filled with art. And thus the children also may see what an impact this person made as an artist.

Why Start with a Story, and What Kind of Story Is It?

I start almost all my teaching with story. Story is the way to bring the students in, to wrap yourself around them, to weave in ideas and experiences, to suggest narratives and histories that may illuminate, entrance, and unsettle. When I tell a story in the classroom, I think about my purposes in telling the story, purposes that include but extend beyond the teaching of craft. The narrative poem with which I start the mythology workshop, for instance (Chapter 4), aims to destabilize gender roles and sexual identities, to offer the students more choice in the roles and categories they assume. That purpose, a kind of delicately woven but intense antihomophobia, was as clear in my mind during the composing as was the demonstration of the language and forms of Greek narrative poetry.

For this workshop, the storytelling with which we begin is more informal, but it is still purposeful. Storytelling is an art that helps students access new concepts

(Saccardi 1997). The purpose of this particular storytelling is to excite interest in the images; to reveal information that may help the students understand the images; and to share what it feels like to be in an intimate relationship with the arts. I have described some of Picasso's biography in the Appendix, but I don't want to give this to the children to read. That information is for us. There is a difference between simply giving students factual information, which may mean nothing to them, and showing them through story how such information could matter, how it could deepen their understanding and their connection with the images. That is why I think it is important to choose an artist or images with which you are familiar and feel some connection. Choose Picasso because I am working here to establish that connection. Choose someone else if you already have an intense interest in an artist, or when you do.

Following is the story with which I open this workshop. The storytelling manifests itself as a whole-group, teacher-led conversation in the classroom, and it is meant to share information and model certain ways of thinking. It is about weaving in information about the artist and the images and constructing a sense of what it is like to be in a relationship with the arts. So where I talk about art I am passionate about, substitute a narrative about your own experience with art if you have one that demonstrates that close connection. If you don't yet, then spend some time with these images before beginning the workshop, and share with the students what you are thinking and feeling. The most important thing is to maintain a tone of intensity. These are art objects we want to share with our students, and we are intensely eager to witness their responses and see what they will construct. We are demonstrating an aesthetic experience. We are showing the children what it means to engage with paintings in ways that let us create meaning.

Starting the Story: How We Model Ways of Thinking

When I gather the students together, I tell them that I am hoping to try some new ways to write poetry. I tell them that I am going to show them some paintings, and that we are going to work with these images together, but that I want to start by explaining why painting is so important to me, and why I want it to be important to them. I tell them I hope they will share the art forms that sustain them, and that perhaps later we can bring in the music, the images, or the performances with which they feel an intense connection. I explain that one reason I think the arts are important is that they bring us together, and I want our classroom to be a place where we come together in this way. I am serious. I want to show them how I bring painting into my heart. So, with the students gathered closely around, and with the images either taped up beside me or propped at my feet or in my hands, I begin, saying something like this:

There are paintings I have to visit every few years, the way other people visit family and friends. I miss them. I want to see them. I wonder if they have changed, or if the way I will feel when I am with them will have changed. It is this love for particular paintings, the willingness to wait in lines, to travel to inconvenient places, that drew me to Andy, my husband, who is a painter, and who feels that same love.

When I haven't seen a particular painting in a long time, I feel it pulling me. I am filled with an intense yearning, a longing to be once more in the presence of the painting. And so I set out again, until I am there, and I know again what it means to be there, with that painting. And sometimes I feel I am in the painting, that I can feel the bombs dropping and the women crying, [I show El Guernica] *or that I am on the beach bouncing like a beach ball [I show* Bather with Beach Ball, *Figure 1–6] And for me, that feeling is the same feeling of being in a poem, and when I take those trains and buses to get to a painting, it will be a book of poetry that I carry on my lap.*

That connection is one I feel when I look at the women in Picasso's paintings. Pablo Picasso, the Spanish painter who painted so many of the women he loved and then left. There are some I find especially compelling. Olga, his first wife, the Russian ballerina. Sara, the American who fascinated him, who was already married to a close friend. Marie-Thérèse, the teenage beauty for whom he betrayed and abandoned Olga. Marie-Thérèse, who bore him a daughter and then saw him become absorbed in a new woman. [I hold up all the images together, as a group.]

I look at his paintings of these women, and I see their beauty, and the way he is absorbed in them, and the way he consumes them. And there are so many women, each seeming so sure of herself, so lovely and strong and alone in his sketches and paintings, until slowly, there is less sureness, and other figures intrude, and maybe a painting even suggests more than one woman, as if the artist's attention is wavering, and soon he will move on, full of artistic pain and passion. I don't know these women. I don't know Olga, the Russian ballerina who left the stage, and married Picasso, and bore him a son. I don't know what she was feeling, in those paintings that show her poised, alone, and elegant. [Show image: Portrait of Olga in an Armchair, *Figure 1–3.] I don't know what she felt when she saw those sketches of their American friend Sara, as a relaxed and confident mother, so different from Olga's formal stiffness. [Show image:* Woman in White, *Figure 1–4]. I don't know how Olga felt when the paintings of Marie-Thérèse Walters, who was not even twenty, began to appear, Marie-Thérèse on that same beach, Marie-Thérèse, a bouncing companion, young, and sure, and finally centered on the canvas [show image:* Bather with Beach Ball, *Figure 1–6].*

But I can imagine it. I can imagine what Olga felt, when she saw herself portrayed on the canvas as a monster, as an insect. (Show image: Seated Bather, *Figure 1–5). I can imagine the shock, and I take some satisfaction in knowing that Picasso, in making those paintings, did not only express his own rage at Olga, but made her enduring, and I think she has a certain power, on the canvas, that he can never remove. I look at these women in Picasso's paintings, and it seems to me that in poetry we can try to express in writerly ways the beauty, the loneliness, and the anguish that are evoked in these paintings.*

And there are other women in Picasso's paintings, and for some of them, he seems to grieve as if he is painting the sorrow of the world. [Show image: El Guernica]. *He tears their bodies in his paintings as they are torn by bombs, he uses these women as figures of suffering, and of grace. And these paintings remind me that when the world seems dark and we cannot make sense of it, art sustains us—it is art that will help us find a light in that darkness, if only by showing us that such a light exists. I see that light most clearly in poetry and in painting, and it is a brilliant, sustaining force. It is that light I want us to kindle in our classroom, that I hope you will carry in this world.*

(*Note:* Please remember to visit the website at *www.heinemann.com/ehrenworth* to access all of these images in color!)

Immersing the Children in Painting and Poetry

You can see I am serious with the children. I want them to care. I want them to see that there are things to love in the world. I want to let them see my aesthetic experience so that they will be eager to make their own. Now the children are also a little familiar with the images, so they seem less intimidating. And they know my expectations for this work. I could also have shown the children how published writers have responded to paintings. If this workshop is part of a larger exploration of poetry, then early in the study, when we read other poems, we'll read some written in response to paintings. One of my favorites is Billy Collins' "Metropolis," from the collection *The Art of Drowning* (1995), because he shows what it is

FIGURE 1–3   *Portrait of Olga in an Armchair,* Picasso

FIGURE 1–4   *Woman in White,* Picasso

FIGURE 1–5   Seated Bather, Picasso   FIGURE 1–6   Bather with Beach Ball, Picasso

like to be intimate with painting, to really notice details like "the glint of candle-light on a silver spoon." I might ask the students to imagine what the paintings that stimulated the poem might look like. We may do some watercolors and create the gallery that the poet might have been in when he wrote. Another favorite is "Fishing on the Susquehanna in July," also by Billy Collins, from *Picnic, Lightning,* (1998). In this poem he is driven by the force of a painting in a museum in Phila-delphia to imagine himself fishing on this faraway river in "a small green flat-bot-tom boat."

If we have lots of time for a poetry study, we might read and paint for several class periods, simply absorbed in poetry and imagery, letting the language wash over us, establishing intimacy with paintings and with published poets, imagin-ing the relation between the languages of painting and poetry, reading aloud, no-ticing what poets noticed in paintings or what happened to them when they looked at paintings. Another great poem that responds to painting is "Big French Bread," by Marvin Bell. It is written in response to the mixed-media relief paint-ing *French Bread,* by Red Grooms, and, with a reproduction of the painting, is in *Heart to Heart: New Poems Inspired by Twentieth Century American Art* (Greenberg 2001). In the painting, an enormous blue-clad figure strides down a French street carrying a baguette, while behind him the street awakens, including a redhead in the background who flings open her shutters, inspiring Bell to write "he loves his bread as the redhead loves the light." It is a good poem for walking in the poet's footsteps as he imagines the experiences of the people in the painting. From that same collection I also really like "Woman at the Piano," by William Jay Smith, a poem inspired by Elie Nadelman's sculpture of the same name. From a simple sculpture of a woman smiling as she plays an upright piano, the poet imagines that when she played, "the fish came flying out of the sea, the mountains knelt, the birds went wild." There is a kind of whimsy to the poem that reflects that of the sculpture.

It is wonderful to be able to really revel in poetry. If you have some space in the curriculum, then take your time reading lots of poetry before writing, so the language and forms will be in the children's minds when they sit down finally to write. In *Weaving in the Arts*, Blecher and Jaffee (1998) describe how their own writing changed when Tom Romano simply read poetry to them every morning. But don't despair if you are trying this workshop as a stand-alone poetry workshop. It still works. You can substitute intensity for long-term immersion. One of the primary purposes of this workshop, in fact, is to create entry points for writing that begin with *looking* rather than reading. So we want to maintain our emphasis on the evocative force of the images. We want to focus the students' attention on the images, and we want to help them construct their responses as poetry. And the children make rather remarkable intuitive leaps. It is possible that we might even get more surprising poems if we don't give the students so many models. Consider these poems written by Carrie (introduced earlier) in response to two of Picasso's portraits of Olga (see Figures 1–7 and 1–8 for her interpretations of the portraits):

Olga

On the canvas
my hair is smooth and long,
my arms white
and my lips red.
How long will
Picasso think I'm beautiful?

Olga

When did I become a monster?
Jagged bones,
an insect's head.
You gave me a skeleton
but no heart.
You have devoured me.

Expecting the Children to Have Aesthetic Responses to Painting and Poetry

Carrie's poems emerged in a middle school writing class where we had only an hour and a half of work time, including looking at the paintings and crafting our poems. I introduced Picasso and the images and then simply put up some slides and handed out some cards. Carrie chose these two to look at. She wrote down what she saw and wondered as she looked at the paintings. And then Carrie worked her looking into poetry. She arranged her noticings and questions in two

FIGURE 1–7   Olga in Armchair, (Carrie's drawing)

columns. Then in conference with me, she worked to revise punctuation choices and create line breaks that made her poems more graceful. It is this side-by-side interaction that really lets us teach the individual writer. And there they were, two poems of rather startling beauty.

A reluctant reader but a close observer, Carrie benefited from an entry point to writing that began with looking. She looked carefully at the paintings, and by following my lead in how I talked about paintings, she simply wrote down what she saw and what it made her think. This seems like simple work, but really this work is the mark of Carrie's aesthetic experience with the paintings. Sometimes we look at paintings to see the artist's view. Carrie, however, looked at the paintings and imagined how Olga viewed her world.

Carrie was thirteen years old. She didn't know how Picasso sought Olga, or if he adored her while she was with child. Carrie didn't know in what ways Picasso was unfaithful to Olga, she didn't know what it was like when he brought Marie-Thérèse to the beach, or in what ways Picasso came to abhor and abandon Olga. Carrie was thirteen and did not know these things. But she could imagine them. She could see them evoked, mysterious, partial, in the paintings. Eisner asks: "What does it mean to secure poetic meaning, and what does poetic meaning help one to understand?" (1994, 19). Carrie secured poetic meaning. She envisioned the moment portrayed in the painting and all that it implied for this woman's past and future. Carrie came to know these things through looking, through participating in the paintings. And she came to know on the page, so that as we read her poems, our perspective shifts to Olga. Carrie's writing reminds us of the profound empathy of which children are capable, and of the ways we perhaps underestimate the knowledges of early adolescence.

Teaching Children to Look Closely

Carrie wrote these poems from slides, which were what I had available at the time. When we look at images with children, either the images need to be large enough that the class may see them clearly or the students need their own copies

FIGURE 1–8   *Seated Bather,* (Carrie's drawing)

to examine closely. I have had large color copies made of these four portraits, and I laminated them, which is also how you can often purchase images from museum bookshops. With the images in front of us and with some idea of Picasso's relationship to these women in the students' minds, now is when we practice looking closely and interpreting our observations as craft. I may introduce an observation record sheet to help the students notice form, color, composition (some of the craft of painting). A blank observation record sheet is available in the Appendix, on page 131. I usually like to begin by looking at one pair of images together with the children as a large group, so that I can model how to relate what we notice with ideas about artistic craft and choice.

The most vivid comparison to model with is *Olga in an Armchair* and *Seated Bather*, so I may begin with those two. Looking at *Olga in an Armchair*, I talk about and record notes on the elegant curves of the lines of her dress and her arm, the restrained colors, the whiteness of her skin and the darkness of her dress. I notice her gaze—the way she looks not quite at the viewer and artist. I think about what makes her seem so feminine and contained—what it is about her pose and her attire that suggest how the artist sees her. If they haven't noticed it, I'll push the children to observe her location on the canvas, how she seems nudged to one side, and how the painting was never finished, as if having captured her likeness, Picasso abandoned interest. This observation takes time; we might spend half an hour just on this image. The children join in, but I am also unafraid to show them what they have not noticed. It takes practice to look closely.

Then we look at *Seated Bather*, another portrait of Olga. We look at the jagged lines, the monstrous forms, the way the head looks like a praying mantis, the insect that eats her mate after she has coupled with it. We note how Picasso has retained some female, human forms, such as her breasts, but he has distorted them to make them seem monstrous. We see how enormous Olga is now on the canvas, how she seems to fill all the available space in a way that is menacing. We observe how her body looks like a shell or an insect form. We think about how quiet the colors are and how that almost makes her monstrosity more shocking. I want the children to see that abstracted forms can demonstrate a lot of artistic choice—they are not random marks. We think about how Picasso might have felt about Olga and what might have made him want to paint her like that. We wonder what Olga might have felt when she saw the painting. We compare it with the earlier image.

Recording Our Observations in Ways That Help Us Write

So I am moving from a kind of shared reading of the painting, where I am doing the looking and speaking, to an interactive reading, where the children participate, and then I will have the children continue and practice looking with these two images by recording all their observations in notes. I often use observation record sheets for this work because I can nudge the children to look closely by asking questions. Also, it organizes the children's noticings in a way that makes it easy to confer with them later when they are trying to write poems. Here are fourteen-year-old Johanna's observation sheets, for example:

Observation Record Sheet
Title: *Olga in an Armchair*

1. How does Picasso portray Olga in this painting? Write down words or phrases that you think of as you look at her and support them with evidence in the painting:
  elegance—still posture, draped positioning on the chair
  beauty—grace with her hand drooping, red lips, white skin
  sophistication—the hair tied back, the makeup, the flowing dress
  intensity—the eyes, the stiffness, seems formal
  importance—because he loves her?

2. Try to describe the forms and colors that shape Olga and what they suggest:
tan background, the figure is mostly black—contrast
the shadows in the background—sense of mystery, shape her
black—sadness? formal? folds in the dress are parallel with her neck line
her position—feminine? but tight? holding back?
contrast white face and dark eyes and rosy cheeks and red lips
eyes—focused on what? Picasso? Seems withdrawn. Looks through him not
   at him

3. How do you imagine the relationship between the painter and Olga?
She seems hesitant—something in her posture, some way she is tight
She looks outward only a little, concentration, confusion?
Picasso seems enamored of her beauty and elegance, but not of her personality.

Observation Record Sheet
Title: *Seated Bather*

1. How does Picasso portray Olga in this painting? Write down words or phrases that you think of as you look at her and support them with evidence in the painting:
harshness—she looks like a monster. Hideous
an insect or a dinosaur skeleton—all bones
mutation—some of her is bones and some seems to be flesh. Deformed
a fossil—something dead, left over, but still with us. Discarded

2. Try to describe the forms and colors that shape Olga and what they suggest:
she's huge—she fills the whole canvas
jagged edges, sharp teeth.
head like an insect—Praying Mantis—eat their lovers?
solid—like she's not going away. But alone.
watching—her eyes are there, but empty, but she sits like she is watching
empty—this big, empty form, he has eaten her? Will she eat him? Repellent.

3. How do you imagine the relationship between the painter and Olga?
He must hate her. Disgust. He is disgusted
Is he afraid of her?
I wonder if he ever loved her, could you love someone and show them like
   that?
she is the one who won't look at him

It is easier for Johanna to find ways to describe the more abstract *Seated Bather* because she is comparing it to the more formal *Olga in an Armchair*. Comparison is the clearest method to sharpen students' skills in observation and analysis. The students will understand their task much better if they examine two images at once, just as they can compare craft in written text more easily when they have two models to examine. Comparison lifts students out of conversation about content and into conversation about how content is presented (Calkins 1996). I think my job at this stage is to listen, to help them say more, to push them to look closely, and to help them think about why the artist painted in this way and not another. We are helping the children imagine the choices the painter makes, which are similar to those a writer makes. We are encouraging them to articulate the experiences they imagine through the painting. In a way, we are helping them record their aesthetic experience with the painting so that it may lead to writing.

Then I give the students the rest of the images to look at and continue this work. I may remind the students who Sara is, that she is the married friend who stayed on the same beach with Picasso and Olga. The married mother whom Picasso painted again and again, as if fascinated with her beauty or something hidden in her. (Sara and her husband were the prototypes for F. Scott Fitzgerald's novel *Tender Is the Night*). And I may remind them who Marie-Thérèse is, that she is the new love, the young love who appears on the beach with Picasso while Olga is abandoned, and that for a time Picasso is painting both women, Olga in monstrous forms and Marie-Thérèse in playful ones.

I have the students work in small groups or partnerships and I confer, helping them, if necessary, think about how the rounded, bouncy forms of the *Bather with Beach Ball* evoke a playful, joyful mood very different from the tension induced by the rough, jagged forms of the *Seated Bather*. The work you do looking at form here will stay with the students when they look at visual and written imagery in the future. In my conferring, I push the students to use language that is picturesque, to choose words that mirror the forms in the paintings. We notice that words that mean harsh things often have harsh sounds, just as forms can be harsh or smooth, jagged or bouncy.

When the students have had work time to look closely and to record their observations, we come together to share our observations. We may make a chart of words and phrases for each painting. We may reproduce in drawing some of the lines and forms, as Carrie did in her sketches of the paintings. We may record questions that are raised by the paintings, things we wonder about. If the students want to continue this work with more images, I give them postcards or reproductions now, and I may give them some related information for these images. I have found that telling just a tiny story creates a context for the images that helps the children become intimate with them quickly. I bring out more images, though, only when I am sure the children are *good* at looking. There is something rich in having the students all look at different images, but initially you need to scaffold their endeavors. By having all the students focus their attention on just a few images, such as these four by Picasso, you can easily tell the story to support the images, and in sharing observations and responses, the children create a deep pool of written observations to draw on when they begin writing poetry.

Freewriting and Drafting: Expecting the Children to Write

Our next step is to move from looking to writing poems. When students seem ready, I ask them to look over their observation sheets to find any phrases or questions or words that they may want to use when they write. Then I simply say that we are going to freewrite some poems as notebook entries, or as entries that could turn into poems. Their writing can be a response to what they see, a descriptive response. Or they can imagine the experience of the artist or the sitter. Or they can do both of these or something else. These are simply unfettered freewrites with the paintings as prompts. Linda Rief describes the freewriting process as a way to help writers get started and develop fluency, and it is effective, especially when practiced often (1992). The students will return to some of these initial freewrites. They select beginnings to draft from, or they lift out words or phrases they like and start again. In the intimate conversations I have with individual students, I can help them see the possibilities in some of these choices. On the other hand, of course, a student may draft a finished poem on the first try. As Pulitzer prizewinner Don Murray (1968) reminds us, there is no one writing process. If the students turn to their notebooks easily, I just let them go, and I'll sit and work on a poem also.

I don't supply a mentor text because I want the children's writing to come from their interaction with the images, not from another piece of writing. If any of the children are stuck, or can't quite envision what a poem might look like, I might share some poetry, but it won't be poetry about these particular images. I might read aloud the poem in *You Hear Me?* called "Does My Mother Look Like This?" written by a fourteen-year-old boy who imagines what his mother looks like. He asks if her face shows a person "who would leave four sons and a daughter and go to another place?" It is a poem that shows how simple and brief a poem may be and still be very affecting. I am hesitant, though, to do much or any reading at this stage. Many reluctant writers are also reluctant readers, and reading more with them doesn't always help; sometimes it intimidates them. Instead, I will look over each student's shoulder, read some of what has been written, and remind the students that they have already been writing. They can look at their observation sheets and start with one noticing, or one question, or one word, and write from there.

If we look closely at Johanna's freewrite for a poem, for instance, we can see how it emerges directly from the noticings she made on her observation sheets about the images of Olga seated in an armchair and as the monstrous bather. It was in looking that she did most of her writing:

Olga

through his eyes
she is beautiful
she is grace
he is enamored

he paints her
because she is important
she is important
because *he* loves her

she looks through him
hesitant
she holds back
does she love him?

he looks at her
but does not see *her*

what he sees is hideous
it is deformed
he is disgusted

his brush exposes her
she is revealed—
teeth, bones, shell
she is repellent now

she has been discarded
alone with the sea
rejected to emptiness
she will not look at him again

Johanna has relocated many of her noticings directly into this freewrite. By centering them on the page and breaking the lines into short phrases, she makes them *look* like a poem. These are easy craft moves to teach children, especially in conferring, when we can really look closely with them at their writing. On the first day of writing, I nudge some students to share at the end of the class. This gives us the opportunity to have a conversation about these moves, and about what students are trying to do in their poetry, and where we are getting stuck, if we are getting stuck. Usually we have to look again at the images and see if we are calling them up in our poetry, if we are paying enough attention. I might share some student writing such as Carrie's and have the children see where in the images she got her ideas. We may also talk about ways to revisit what they have written so far. These include taking a word or line they really like and starting a new poem with that phrase or selecting words or phrases from several freewrites and reworking them in a single poem. Conferring at this stage is all about maintaining enthusiasm for writing. It is about paying close attention to what each child is doing in her writing and naming it in a way that lets the child see what she is doing that is powerful or potentially powerful.

Craft and Revision

So what may the class look like now? Some students are drafting more poems while others are drafting their first ones. If this is part of a larger poetry workshop, some will be working on these poems related to Picasso, and others may choose to revisit poems they wrote in other ways. It is always a balance between creating as much opportunity for choice as possible and teaching the children things we think will widen these choices. When the students have some drafts, when they have decided to some extent what they want to say, I look at craft choices with them. We may turn to the poems in *Heart to Heart: New Poems Inspired by Twentieth Century American Art* to read poems written in the presence of painting, and we may look at their craft. We may go back to Billy Collins. Or I might interrupt their writing to read some poems of love. With my high school classes I like to read Elizabeth Barrett Browning's "Sonnet XIV" from *Sonnets from the Portuguese* (1902), which begins "if thou must love me, let it be for naught except love's sake only." We talk about the nature of love, and what kind of love she wants, and what she might have to say about Picasso's love, as demonstrated in these paintings.

Again, in this workshop I select the things to read with care and I keep them minimal. Maureen Barbieri showed me that it is perfectly possible to look at a single poem such as "Big French Bread" and think about word choice, and line breaks, and imagery, and repetition, and punctuation, and spacing on the page, and almost all the craft lessons we want to teach in one workshop. *A Note Slipped Under the Door* (Flynn and McPhillips 2000) is a lovely guide to teaching the craft of poetry if you want some guidance in this area.

With some thinking about craft fresh in our heads, we turn to revision. We choose one draft to revise, and we revisit it, thinking about structure, and line breaks, and word choice, and spacing, and the things that poets may think about when they discipline their poems so that they are things of beauty and clarity. I remind the children that their poems are also images and will provoke aesthetic responses in particular ways. Carrie's draft, for example, looked like this:

Olga 1

On the canvas my hair is smooth and long
my arms white—and lips red
 How long will Picasso think I'm beautiful?

Olga 2

When did I become a monster?
jagged bones—and an insect head
You gave me a skeleton but no heart
You have devoured me

Conferring with Carrie was about helping her *see* her poems. I asked her to think about whether it would make a difference if the poems looked and sounded symmetrical. She decided to shift them so they read across from each other, which also helped her make her titles and phrasing more graceful. I showed her how sometimes poets make line breaks so that each line is a single image; this is a more elegant way to separate images than a dash. I asked her where she wanted her reader to pause, to breathe, and as she read them aloud, I marked her page for her. Carrie rewrote her poems, making the line breaks you see on page 30, and then she could *see* that she had to make the punctuation coherent. Revising poetry for Carrie was about paying attention to clarity and beauty in how the poems sounded and how they looked. And so she came to the poems as they look on page 30 in their final form.

It is helpful if students share their poems as they work on craft; we have a kind of poetry crucible in which the students may forge other poems or refine their originals. I like to write their poems on large sheets of paper so that we can see what they look like as well as hear them. With poetry, it matters what the words look like on the page. Then we may revise others, or we may turn to more images and do more writing. I confer, confer, confer, and only return to whole-class craft minilessons if it seems like the whole group would benefit. And sometimes the children can give these lessons. When Carrie demonstrated how she revised her poem, she helped her classmates, for instance. The workshop, thus, may be a few days, or it may extend longer and you may find the students doing more of the teaching and conferring, until that exultant moment when everyone has a poem or poems to celebrate.

Celebration: Publishing the Poems and Naming Our Work

I call this part of the workshop celebration because we celebrate our involvement with these images, and we celebrate the poems that emerge. We could call this part publishing, but that would only be part of what we are doing. Shelley Harwayne taught me to name with students what it is that they can do at the end of any work, so that they will carry it with them. I name them as students who are becoming art experts. They know how to look closely. They know how to ask questions that lead them to secure meaning. I name us as a community that cares about and is involved with the arts. I name our classroom as a place where we are able to come together around the arts and where we may envision how to bring a larger community together. We may have a gallery opening of our poems, with the paintings. We write our poems in beautiful letters and put them up in a hall of the school with the paintings beside them. We may widen our poetic interest in the arts. We may decide to move to music and to write poetry from musical prompts. We may bring in dance performances. We are looking to extend the boundaries of our experience, looking for ways of living as well as ways of writing.

FIGURE 1–9   Bather with Beach Ball, (Carrie's drawing)

I want to bounce on the beach
like a ball
across the sand
with the ocean behind me
and the blue, blue sky
your hair will blow
and I will blow kisses
come bounce with me
and bring sand into the house

If we have been writing many poems, another way to celebrate our work is to create poetry books or anthologies. Judy Davis of Manhattan New School, for instance, is renowned in the city for her illustrated poetry books (Davis and Hill 2003). Starting with a bare book, a bound book of heavy white paper, the students include published poems and their own responses, and they illustrate the books in watercolor or other media. They are simply lovely. For this workshop we could make this kind of book with reproductions or drawings of the paintings accompanied by the children's poems. One advantage of a student-made poetry book is that, if you need a vehicle for assessment, you can create a rubric for it, something that includes, for instance, timeliness; visual design and presentation; clarity of the introduction; articulateness of the poems; and perhaps risk-taking as a writer. Or we can say that grading poetry is anathema and assess the students as writers on perseverance and individual growth instead.

IMPLICATIONS: RECOGNIZING MEANINGFUL WORK IN TEACHING POETRY

There will always be poems that let us see that this work is working. There is an example of one of these poems on page 40. It shows me that painting does reach young children. It shows me that looking at painting stimulates children to imagine visual and emotional landscapes. It shows that writing through the visual arts can help children write in evocative ways. It is a thing of great joy and beauty. It was written by a fifth grader named Nelson. (See also Carrie's drawing of *Bather with Beach Ball* in Figure 1–9, the reproduction on page 29, and the color image available through the website.)

It is rather beautiful that when Picasso made this painting, he put joy into the world, and that when Nelson looks at it, he creates a poem that also puts joy into the world. Picasso's painting and Nelson's poem are bouncy and full of air. Both are aesthetic invitations. They say, "Come bounce with me."

Nelson lives in the projects. In his notebook, Nelson writes that he hasn't ever been to the beach, but he thinks from the painting that it must be a place where you go with people who love you. We can't go to the beach, but when we say we are going to the museum, Nelson stands up on his chair and shouts "Yay!"

REFERENCES

Angelou, M. 1969/1993. *I Know Why the Caged Bird Sings*. New York: Bantam.

Blecher, S., and K. Jaffee. 1998. *Weaving in the Arts: Widening the Learning Circle*. Portsmouth, NH: Heinemann.

Browning, E. B. 1902. *Sonnets from the Portugese*. New York: G. P. Putnam's Sons.

Calkins, L. 1996. *The Art of Teaching Writing*. Portsmouth, NH: Heinemann.

Chabon, M. 2000. *The Adventures of Kavalier and Clay*. New York: Picador.

Collins, B. 1995. *The Art of Drowning*. Pittsburgh: University of Pittsburgh Press.

———. 1998. *Picnic, Lightning*. Pittsburgh: University of Pittsburgh Press.

Davis, J. and S. Hill. 2003. *The No-Nonsense Guide to Teaching Writing: Strategies, Structures, and Solutions*. Portsmouth, NH: Heinemann.

Dewey, J. 1934/1980. *Art as Experience*. New York: Perigee.

Eisner, E. 1994. *Cognition and Curriculum Reconsidered*. 2d ed. New York: Teachers College Press.

Fagin, L. 2000. *The List Poem: A Guide to Teaching and Writing Catalog Verse*. New York: Teachers and Writers Collaborative.

Flynn, N., and S. McPhillips. 2000. *A Note Slipped Under the Door*. Portland, ME: Stenhouse.

Franco, B., ed. 2000. *You Hear Me? Poems and Writings by Teenage Boys*. Cambridge, MA: Candlewick.

Greenberg, J., ed. 2001. *Heart to Heart: New Poems Inspired by Twentieth Century American Art*. New York: Abrams.

Greene, M. 2000. "Lived Spaces, Shared Spaces, Public Spaces." In *Construction Sites: Excavating Race, Class, and Gender Among Urban Youth,* ed. M. Fine and L. Weiss, 293–304. New York: Teachers College Press.

Hejinian, L. 2000. *The Language of Inquiry*. Berkeley: University of California Press.

Murray, D. 1968. *A Writer Teaches Writing*. Portsmouth, NH: Heinemann.

Nye, N. S. 2002. *The Flag of Childhood*. New York: Aladdin Paperbacks.

Rief, L. 1992. *Seeking Diversity*. Portsmouth, NH: Heinemann.

Rubin, W., ed. 1996. *Picasso and Portraiture*. New York: Museum of Modern Art.

Saccardi, M. 1997. *Art in Story: Teaching Art History to Elementary School Children*. North Haven, CT: Linnet.

Stafford, W. 1996. *Even in Quiet Places*. Lewiston, ID: Confluence.

WEBSITES WITH PICASSO IMAGES

www.moma.org/   The Museum of Modern Art, New York.

www.artchive.com/artchive/ftptoc/picasso_ext.html Click on different periods in Picasso's career and get a summary of each period, as well as links to particular images reproduced online.

www.artcyclopedia.com/artists/picasso_pablo.html Master site with links to museum pages with online Picasso images. A terrific source leading to all the major museum sites around the world.

The 1997 exhibition at the Boston Museum of Fine Arts of the first decade and a half of the painter's career. The site continues to maintain a time line, some biographical information, and some images.

www.art.com/   Sells posters online, including many Picasso images of women.

Chapter Two

American Landscape and the Aesthetic Experience

These are my favorite museum rooms,
the out-of-the-way ones on the upper floors,
usually unpeopled except for a single guard
who appears and disappears in the maze of walls
where these minor American paintings are hung.
—Billy Collins

It is a marvelous thing to see children figuratively enter American landscape paintings in their writing. There is something about how large the landscapes are, how detailed and yet how vast the scenes are, that allows not merely a single child but a social group to enter a single painting, to move about the painting in their narratives, and even to come upon each other in their narratives. It is a participatory way of looking and writing peculiarly apt to landscape and narrative. There are three ways I want to describe here to engage students with American landscape paintings in order to write. Each of these ways functions as an alternate entry point to writing that begins with looking, each of these ways also engages with certain moments in American history through looking, and each of these ways asks the students to experiment with certain rigorous and contained narrative writing. These ways of looking and writing are (1) taking the scene in a painting as a remembered vignette; (2) writing a historical journal set within a landscape; and (3) assuming a role in a painting of a historical event.

In each of these endeavors we engage students with a painting in order to write and also in order to engage the faculties of observation, imagination, and interpretation. It is work that we may pursue in the social studies or humanities class, but its implications expand to all aspects of literacy, including how we notice detail and patterns, how we question what we see, and how we express our response in writing by describing both what we come to notice and the implications of this noticing. It is a way of writing that carries with it a sense of responsibility and a sense of purpose. It helps point the children outward at the same time that it values inner experiences.

CHILDREN ENGAGING WITH AMERICAN LANDSCAPE PAINTING

When I first witnessed Tamara and Felicia, two fifth graders, imagining themselves coming upon each other in Thomas Cole's painting *The Oxbow*, I was astonished. It was an aesthetic experience, in the sense of an experience that we cannot predict, where we engage with a work of art and something unexpected and transformative occurs. I think part of what happens is that we practice close observation, which we don't really do too often in the ordinary transactions of day-to-day living. When we engage with painting, we slow down. We look closely. We notice detail, we wonder about purpose, and we begin to participate in the painting. We bring the art of ourselves, our autobiography, to the experience of a painting or sculpture. I think of the aesthetic experience as one of transference and of immanence. We look to know more about the world as shown by this artist, and we also look to know more about ourselves in relation to this vision.

I have come to realize that we cannot teach aesthetic experiences. But we can try to orchestrate them, and we can engage one kind of art, painting, with another of the arts, writing, and make writing itself an aesthetic experience, a way of engaging with the world. When I think about what really matters in writing and in literacy, it is that literacy is a way we articulate what we know and what we imagine. When we look in order to write, we practice looking closely and imaginatively. I want to show here what happens in this aesthetic writing experience, including the ways children imagine landscapes other than those they have known, the ways they transfer visual knowledge into their writing, and the ways the experience helps them articulate in writing their sense of the world and their place in it.

The painting becomes part of the experience we bring to the writing. What we see, what we wonder, becomes what in other writing and reading practices we may call prior knowledge. It is *from* the painting that we build knowledge. And with this knowledge, a way of knowing a certain scene from looking at it and thinking within it, we activate a sense of our own history and we imagine a particular point of view that I think of as the convergence of the personal, the observed, the historical, and the imagined. The children do not need to know American history or painting in order to write. They *come to know* through writing. And because it is a coming to know that happens through engaging with the arts, it is a coming to know that is uniquely aesthetic and lasting. "Art is long," says Dewey in *The School and Society* (1900/1990, 104). We don't forget an aesthetic experience.

WHY AMERICAN LANDSCAPE PAINTING?

Museum-goers rarely visit American landscape paintings. The Impressionist wing will be full, the Egyptian collection will be buzzing, but the paintings in the American collection hang alone in what Billy Collins calls the "unpeopled upper floors." It is hard to remember that when Thomas Cole and Frederick Church painted the Hudson River in the nineteenth century, and when they and their cohort of adventurer-painters ventured farther west to paint the Rockies, people flocked to the galleries in New York and Boston to see their paintings. A single landscape painting, monumental in scale, might be exhibited within a massive wooden frame in a gallery. Visitors could look through view-scopes, narrow tubes that allowed the viewer to peruse the painting as if it were a real landscape. This was the first sight of the West for most viewers. The magnificence of it sustained a belief in manifest destiny, the idea that God intended Americans to conquer and inhabit the West. These paintings are incredibly rich sites for writing because of the enormous scope of the landscape, their attention to detail, and their covert symbolism. The artists who made them were serious about their purpose. They wanted to inspire awe. They wanted to entice. They wanted to instruct. They wanted to define. This means we have so much to see, and there are so many possible interpretations of these paintings.

When we look at a painting with students, we are reading it as we would a text. It helps children if we do this aloud often, so that it becomes natural to say what we see. It is very much like interpreting a poem. Artists make choices just as writers do. So, as you would start with a text by retelling it, maybe using the "chunk and retell" technique, start by describing what you see. And then wonder about the implications of what you see. If the mountains are low and purple and far off, the artist creates a sense of great distance and space. If they tower over the scene, then they give a feeling of power, and even of claustrophobia. They may make the human presence seem small and vulnerable. Lightning and storms and giant waves also threaten the human presence. Rivers disappearing over rocky ledges and forest paths that lead into darkened tunnels give a sense of the unknown. Dappled sunlight and cultivated fields are domestic, and perhaps comforting. Look at imagery just as you would look at language in a poem. Think: What is its effect?

Hudson River School painters, as these nineteenth-century painters who depicted the grandeur of the American landscape were called, were adept at incorporating an iconography, or program of symbolism, of God's power in their landscape paintings. The blasted tree, symbol of the great destructive power of nature and of God. The ominous coming thunderstorm, the passing thunderstorm, the clear blue skies of hope and grace. The cultivated landscape of man's dominion over nature, dotted with churches to show his harmony with God and the natural world, and the dark, untamed wilderness of the West, where (certain chosen) Americans must bring God. Glimpse Hudson River School paintings of the American West and glimpse a nineteenth-century white man's belief in his patriarchal heritage, in the supremacy of the Christian Church, and in the manifest destiny of America as a subjugator of lands and peoples. It is a grand and sweeping vision that acted to overwrite the story lines of those who had a natural claim to the land. It explains a little about how this nation has thought about itself and about how we make history in the ways we choose to record it.

I often feel as if I could teach the history of American history simply in front of a Hudson River School painting of the American West, especially the paintings by Cole, or Church, or Bierstadt, the acknowledged leaders of this school of painting. The paintings express such longing, such yearning, such maniacal grandeur. It is a history of glorifying, of wanting, and of taking. It is a visual history, for instance, that co-opted notions of the American Indian as picturesque. The murderous attacker, the player of games, the crafty woodsman, the tamer of horses, and the gentle family group became part of a Western myth of the noble savage, a way of romanticizing the antagonist even in the act of destroying him. These paintings were viewed as cultural artifacts, and ideas of their significance grew as they came to replace the original subjects, who were displaced in various ways.

And always, visions of the West in all its magnificence enthralled city dwellers and statesmen. Raging waterfalls, snowy peaks, endless plains. In an age before photography was common, people entered the West first through paintings and the etchings that were made from them for the press. Hudson River School painters often painted themselves into these scenes. The small figure of the painter, working at his easel regardless of personal danger or discomfort, hunkered down below towering mountains while storms gathered in the background, was a direct comment upon American manhood. Along with the enticement of natural beauty and unconquered territories, these paintings constructed notions of masculinity as the pursuit of adventure, exploration, and conquest.

There is a way in which to look at Hudson River School paintings as a master narrative, a vision America was creating for itself in the nineteenth century. They mark the shift from a colonial perspective, through the uncertainty of the Civil War, to a new sense of the United States as a nation with the potential to unite the land between two oceans. And it is significant, I am sure, how overwhelming the interest is in the land itself, as if the inhabitants did not signify. The grandeur of the American landscape came to symbolize notions of America as a place of power. The book *Undaunted Courage* by Stephen Ambrose (1996) brings alive some of the sentiments of this era. Ambrose describes how President Thomas Jefferson became enthralled with the idea of exploring the West in order to obtain it, and thus how Merriwether Lewis and William Clark captained the expedition up the Missouri River and over the Rockies to the Pacific. It is a heroic tale, but throughout it Ambrose also tells smaller tales, such as how Lewis used the Shoshone, how he ignored their hunger and their need, seeing only how these Native Americans could be of use to him and his expedition. We see this same urge toward mastery in the paintings.

Hudson River School painters claimed and domesticated the land with their paintbrushes. When we enter these paintings to write, we revisit the land as it was seen when it was thought to be new. We bring to it the same uncertainty and will to learn that nineteenth-century painters, explorers, and viewers did. We may also bring to it new visions that will make the perspective of these paintings less epic and more personal. We will tell the story in other ways and make new histories possible with our stories.

WRITING REMEMBERED SCENES FROM AMERICAN LANDSCAPE PAINTING

Along with the monumental scenes of the West, the Hudson River School painters also painted quieter scenes, of the marshes of the New Jersey shoreline, the boats sailing up and down the Hudson, bringing goods and people to towns along the river, and the small farms of New Hampshire and Massachusetts. The success of such masters as Thomas Cole and Frederick Church encouraged others to celebrate the American landscape in paintings that were more intimate, of smaller scale, such as those that could hang in a house or a tavern. It is these more domestic paintings that we can make the sites of vignettes written as remembered scenes. The smaller size and more intimate scenery of these paintings inspire an intimate engagement with them, a kind of seeking to inhabit the painting as we come to know it. We will literally place ourselves into the painting, or at the edge of the painting, as we imagine the scenery as one that we once inhabited or continue to inhabit.

This kind of engagement demands that we activate our imaginations in response to what we see. That is one reason to try this way of looking and writing: it demands an act of the imagination. It is also a way to create validity, and a sense of solid setting, in any writing that includes a historical perspective. This might include historical fiction or multigenre projects, the exploration in many genres of a critical moment or character, described by Tom Romano in *Blending Genre, Altering Style* (2000) and Camille Allen in *The Multigenre Research Paper* (2001). The painting becomes our setting, and in describing it, young writers learn what it feels like to have a visual in our mind that we are trying to re-create for the reader. I have found that the exercise also helps writers learn to focus on detail and incorporate detail so that it is meaningful in creating a tone or sense of atmosphere. Does the sunlit path entice us? Does it create a feeling that we may wander and roam? We experiment with how details suggest vignette elements. The buildings depicted in the painting are not those of a stranger; we imagine them as ours, and we can consider the implications for our lives. The wind blowing across the canvas is the wind biting at our nose. The deer at the edge of the clearing is one we saw, once, when we were in these woods, by chance, alone.

If the children have access to a public collection, then we write in the museum or gallery. Otherwise, we write from postcards and library books or posters. Two glorious books for images of American landscapes are *American Sublime: Landscape Painting in the United States 1820–1880*, by Wilton (2002) and *All That is Glorious Around Us: Paintings from the Hudson River School*, by Driscoll (1997). Less comprehensive, but also less expensive, is Minks' *Hudson River School* (2002). You can also access the American collection at the website of the Metropolitan Museum, *www.metmuseum.org*, where you can download lovely images or purchase cards and posters. I put up posters and scatter postcards and books and color printouts across the desks so that the children can look through them. They need time simply to engage with the paintings, to see which landscape calls to them. Sometimes one seems to offer a sense of sanctuary. Sometimes one feels familiar. Sometimes one offers a sense of the unknown or ignites the imagination. The experience varies. Sometimes a child seems to want to enter a painting because he can imagine acting in that painting. Other times a child may simply *want* to be in that place. Art lets us do that, enter places that otherwise might be unknown or unimaginable to us.

When the children have had some time to become familiar with the images, I explain that we will be experimenting with writing imagined vignettes from the paintings. Usually this exercise is part of a unit we may be doing on historical fiction or historically informed multigenre projects, but sometimes we write these vignettes simply as a writing exercise or as part of a whole study of writing from images. These vignettes will be small personal narratives, rich in detail. I usually orally walk the children through a scene first, demonstrating how I may begin with "I remember," and then simply describing what I see in a painting, transforming it with my imagination into my remembered home or a place that sticks in my memory for some reason. Take a moment to look at what you see in the painting, and then describe it not as something you are seeing now in a museum, but as a picture you hold in your mind's eye. *I remember the view from our porch when I was twelve, when the apple orchards were in bloom, and winter snows were melting away, and everything smelled like pink springtime.* I remind the students to incorporate their senses, to imagine what a scene may smell and sound like as well as what it looks like. This practice, of envisioning a scene before them and then transforming it into a setting, is one that may carry over for the children even when they are not in front of a painting, if they learn to picture, notice, and transfer detail.

Ways to Confer with the Children About This Writing

The children may choose to begin with "I remember," and they may envision the painting as their home or as one of their favorite or most visited places. They may be writing about the past as if they remember it, or they may set their vignette in the present tense, but it is an imagined present that takes place in the painting. You can imagine how this exercise stimulates the children's powers of invention. But this invention is not fantasy. It is more disciplined than that, because it also calls upon them to exercise their powers of observation and interpretation. They must observe and include details from the paintings in their vignettes. Just getting them to look closely and describe what they see is an important step. Ask them to keep giving more detail. Ask them what season it seems to be and how they know. Ask them what purpose they think any buildings have, and if the land seems touched by humans, and how.

Then we help them make what they see matter, help them call upon what they know from what they may research, what they observe, and their own autobiographies. The children know about social interactions. They know about families. They have concerns and ideas and knowledge. We can help them extend the boundaries of this knowledge by asking them to engage it in new ways. Ask them if they can imagine being in this scene. What would it feel like? What would they do first? What direction in the painting would they want to move in? Who would they want to bring with them? Have them tell each other about the paintings first, orally, so that they hear what it sounds like to describe the painting. Even starting with "I want to be in this painting because . . ." helps them articulate what it is about the painting that they notice and how it interacts with their own desires.

When the children incorporate their own experiences and desires into these vignettes, they weave a historical imagination with observation and interpretation. They are engaged in an aesthetic experience that brings great complexity to their writing. Miranda, for instance, looks at *Cider Making* (Figure 2–1), by

FIGURE 2–1   Cider Making, Mount

William Sidney Mount, circa 1840, which you can see in color through the links of the companion website (*www.heinemann.com/ehrenworth*). Miranda ponders the scene for a while, tracing parts of it with her fingers, talking over with her sixth-grade classmates and me some of the details she is seeing, like the millstone. Miranda has never been out of Manhattan, and she has not seen the remains of these mills. Miranda is involved in writing a multigenre project about a girl living in historical New England. She wants very much to write about someone who grew up in the country. After looking at the painting for almost thirty minutes, Miranda writes:

> Sometimes, when I see the way the boys and men in our family work, it feels like they get to sit around a lot, and that every time they work, then they get to sit and talk about how hard they work. I remember the day we made cider up on the hill behind the farm where there is a millstone that turns if you hook a horse up to it. I mean, the men made cider. The girls and women woke everyone up and milked the cows and fed the animals and made the butter and did the cooking and wrapped ourselves in blankets and brought the food up the hill to the field and waited for the men to eat and then washed everything and then went back to cleaning the house (inside) and making cheese (in the dairy) and washing all the clothes (in the washroom), including the blankets we got dirty bringing the food to the men, and sewing and sewing and sewing (inside too).
>
> The boys and men made cider. Outside. Outside up on the hill behind the farm where the grass is green, the sun shines and you can see the blue mountains. The air smelled like apples, all soft and fresh. They rolled big barrels around, and pulled the white horse to crush the apples and then they sat around and talked, leaning against the big barrels in the sun, drinking the cider, with the dogs lying around too.

You can see that Miranda has some gender concerns that she is bringing into her vignette. You can also see that she is able to translate these concerns convincingly into a historical moment and that, in fact, the painting gives her a setting in which to voice these concerns. Miranda's writing tells me something about aesthetic experiences. It shows me that we can use them as opportunities for the children to make new observations and engage in new writing experiences. By noticing and including the landscape details of the painting, Miranda is able to ground her story of women's labor. She harnesses the pastoral qualities of the landscape as a way of illuminating her (perhaps romanticized) view of men's historical access to the outdoors and to masculine moments of leisure and companionship. In imagining the life of a rural farm girl, she perhaps also comes to new realizations about herself as a city dweller. She has probably done more, really, than she knows. She responds aesthetically to the painting in implicit ways in her own writing.

Most of the work of Miranda's writing occurred in the noticing stage. I asked the children to describe the painting to someone else in the class, to talk about why they had chosen it, to storytell orally some of what they might write if they used it as a setting. Miranda's first draft had all of the words of this version, but the punctuation and sentence structure were less purposeful. In conferring with her about revision, I talked with Miranda about the power of repetition, and she inserted these rather ironic parenthetical explanations that give a wry tone to her writing. In fact, looking at painting helps us think about tone, or atmosphere, which creates a context for conversation about sentence structure. I think of it like brushstroke—wide and sweeping, or short and controlled, depending on our purpose. Perhaps because Miranda had lots of opportunity to say orally what she saw in the painting, I didn't have to prompt her to notice more detail in revision. She had looked closely and made decisions about which landscape elements would support her purpose. And clearly Miranda had a purpose, one that I wouldn't have thought to direct her toward. I just helped her see that in this piece of writing, she had found a way to ground her gender concerns so that they surfaced naturally within a lyrical description of setting. Having to focus outward on the details of the landscape brought a new subtlety to Miranda's writing.

Will, a seventh grader, doesn't bring a political agenda to the paintings. He is more interested in describing the feeling of what he calls "upness," which he gets when he looks at the distances created in Kensett's 1869 painting *Lake George*, in the Metropolitan (see Figure 2–2; go to *www.heinemann.com/ehrenworth* for a link to a color image of the painting online).

When I ask Will to tell me more about this feeling of upness, he says that it is just "up" in every way. Up in the sky, up in the mountains, up, up is what he feels when he looks at this painting. Like Miranda, in his oral rehearsing of this writing, Will does most of the work that some might think would come later, in revision. When he tells me about what he sees and feels, I ask him to explain how old he is, and if it matters that he is from the city, and if there is any way to hold onto this feeling he gets when he looks at this painting. Will writes:

> I remember, once, when I was thirteen, my Dad took some vacation, and he took me with him to climb to the top of this mountain where there is this lake. When you get to the top of the mountain, everything is kind of gray and cloudy, but not wet like it is going to rain, more wet like you *are* the rain. You are way up in the sky and it is like you are part of the lake and part of the mountain and part of the clouds too. I've always lived in the city, all my life, and I never knew what it felt like, before, to be a cloud. Now when I see the rain in the city, I look at it and I look up, and I think about the lake, and the mountain, and the cloud that I was a part of.

Will may choose to revise this piece further if he incorporates it into the multigenre projects we are working on. But he is a reluctant writer, and I don't

FIGURE 2–2   *Lake George*, Kensett

ask him to do further revision now, choosing instead to celebrate and name what Will is doing. It is truly lovely the way Will re-creates the experience of seeing this painting for the first time, in our classroom, at age thirteen, as a remembered vignette. He weaves this imagined experience so convincingly that it becomes real for him and his audience. In discovering this painting, Will writes a memory into existence, so that his relationship with the rain in our city will never be the same for him or for those of us who read the vignette. In engaging *with* art, Will makes writing an art.

WRITING HISTORICAL JOURNALS SET WITHIN A LANDSCAPE PAINTING

Sometimes the work we do with landscape paintings may be part of a larger historical study. In fact, engaging with paintings is one way to transform the study of American history into engagement with the American experience. The large-scale panoramic views of the Hudson River School painters are particu-

FIGURE 2–3   *View from Mount Holyoke, Northhampton, Massachusetts, After a Thunderstorm—The Oxbow,* Cole

larly enticing for this kind of work. In exploring western expansion, for instance, we see the American landscape as it was seen by some of the first explorers and documenters of that land, and we can experience that vision. We may enter this landscape in order to move around within it, documenting our movement in writing and discovering what it felt like when the land was, indeed, new to the viewers. We may enter it in order to disrupt it, by offering the imagined perspective of those who came before, whose vision existed before these newcomers came to claim the land. Inevitably, the experience becomes one with social implications, as we move either alone or in groups across the land, aware always that the landscape has social significance in terms of settlement, knowledge, and power.

We can engage with any large-scale Hudson River painting for this writing experience. I often start with Thomas Cole's 1836 painting *View from Mount Holyoke, Northhampton, Massachusetts, After a Thunderstorm—The Oxbow* (Figure 2–3). This is a favorite for me because it is large-scale and beautiful and also because it is available through the Metropolitan Museum's website and almost every library book on American landscape painting. When we read the painting, we see that it

FIGURE 2–4   The Oxbow, Cole (detail)

presents the East as a domesticated pastoral landscape dotted with churches and farms and the West, across a river, as a dark and mysterious wilderness of woods and mountains, shrouded in thunderstorms, with evidence of God or nature's power in the trees blasted by lightning. The painting thus embodies American notions of manifest destiny and the romanticizing of the West, and our potential for harmony with nature as symbolic of harmony with God. It also serves as a reminder of God's power over the natural world. It is a detailed yet enigmatic landscape. (Go to *www.heinemann.com/ehrenworth* for links to sites with more details on this work.)

Most often, the work I have done with *The Oxbow* and other monumental landscapes such as Bierstadt's *Rocky Mountains* is part of a study of western expansion, and the students create invented journals of someone who is crossing the Oregon Trail or settling in the frontier. The landscapes thus become one way to imagine and articulate setting. I ask the students to create journal entries from *within* one of the paintings we have available. Students may be anywhere in their chosen painting; they may move around the landscape in their journal entry; they may come upon their classmates. Students in the same painting thus create varied and sometimes interlocking visions and voices from within the same setting.

I begin by just talking with the children about what they see in a painting, using *The Oxbow* as a model. They often describe the cultivated landscape to the east and the wilderness to the west. They see the river as a divider and a path between the two parts. Gradually, they notice the blasted tree which has been destroyed by lightning (see Figure 2–4), and they observe the thunderclouds passing overhead to the west and the sun streaming out in the east. They find houses and orchards and wagons and people in the east.

They find heavy foliage and mysterious dark copses to the west. I explain the symbolism of these elements, and often we'll glance at other Hudson River School landscapes and recognize many of these symbols in them as well. The children enjoy feeling that they have a kind of secret knowledge of pictorial language. And it is a language, one with which children often become remarkably adept. They notice details and imagine their implications, and we can ask them, then, to do so in their writing.

To help the students envision how to create a narrative that takes place within the landscape, I do some interactive storytelling in which I demonstrate how a narrator moves around in a painting. I often prefer storytelling to formal minilessons about *how* to write narrative, as stories are more suggestive and at the same time less directive. I may begin this narrative like this:

This morning Willie and I got caught on the other side of the river and we thought we were never going to make it back to the farm and our momma and poppa. We were playing in the bottom of the boat that Farmer Wilson ties up by the shore. We were playing that we were on our way to New York City, where Aunt Ida says the people all live in sin and filth. Out of nowhere, the sky got all black and the wind whipped up, and the boat just washed out into the water and across the river. I wondered if the thunderstorm were sent as a warning to us for playing that we were going to New York. By the time we reached the middle of the river, it was raining so hard that the boat just started to sink right under us. We tried to swim back to our shore, but I don't swim so good in a dress, and even Willie had a hard time with all his wet clothes, and his boots that he couldn't get off. So we just hung onto the boat, which was just all the way underwater, and it pushed across to the other shore like it was sailing, with the wind howling all the way.

When we felt the shore under us, we were afraid even to get out of the river, because it was like a haunted woods there, it was so dark and scary. There were trees crashing down and branches breaking and flying through the air and it was like we had just been put down in some kind of nightmare. One tree had just been hit by lightning and it was all charred. It made me think what could happen to us if we were struck. Willie tried to pull us up the hill because he thought the river was flooding and we might be drowned. But it was almost impossible to climb because of the bushes, which were all thorny, and they kept scratching us and grabbing at our clothes. Finally I found an old tree trunk that was hollow, and we crawled inside. Imagine my surprise when we heard a noise from the back of the hollow. It was . . .

And so on. I invent narrators who are near the students' age, whose story involves some kind of tension, and that tension is involved with the landscape. I incorporate without fuss some of the symbolic elements, such as the thunderstorm and the blasted tree. Only some children notice this, and often it is not those children who are proficient or public writers and thinkers. Often it is quieter ones who we did not know had these intuitive powers. I ask the children then to say where the characters might move next in the painting, and we tell the story in an interactive manner, pointing out where we are in the painting, practicing how it sounds when a narrator is moving through a landscape. It is amusing and lively, but soon the children realize that they need to look closely and say what they see, and then they are performing oral storytelling, which is rehearsal for writing.

If this is our first experience looking at or writing historical journals, whether real or invented, I may give the students a brief focus lesson on some aspects of historical journals, including the difference between a diary or journal that is contemporary with the events described and a memoir that is written later. Since we are writing invented journals, I ask the students in their entry to show who is writing, to describe the setting (and remember that the painting is their setting), and to document what is happening that day. Before we come to look at the paintings, I may read aloud some excerpts from real journals, such as *Mourt's Relation* (Heath 1986) or the many Oregon Trail diaries available online, and we may also read fictional ones such as *Across the Wide and Lonesome Prairie: The*

Oregon Trail Diary of Hattie Campbell, 1847 (Gregory 1996). If I read these texts, I read them aloud, in order to make them more accessible.

Oral Storytelling and Social Interactions in the Writing Process

Once the students are familiar with the purpose and nature of historical journals, we choose paintings to enter. Before we write, I usually have the students do oral storytelling with a partner. This gives them a chance to rehearse before they write, and it also lets them hear each other's ideas, so that sometimes children choose to be in the same painting together or to react to what happens in someone else's journal entry. This has been one of the most surprising elements of this writing activity for me, seeing how the children engage with each other within the paintings. When she hears her friend's journal entry, one girl comes across the dog who is created in the friend's story. Fifth graders Tamara and Felicia, in their own entries, come upon each other in the woods, so that their journal entries meet and they continue together. They choose, however, to continue to write two separate journals, giving different perspectives on their journey through *The Oxbow* (Figure 2–3). Part of Tamara's journal reads:

> Suddenly when we got to the top of the hill, we saw a man sitting alone in the woods. He was holding something, and I thought maybe it was a weapon, and I thought we should hide in the hollow tree that was behind us. But Felicia told me that he was a painter, and I realized it was Thomas Cole, the famous painter.

Felicia's journal reads:

> When we got to the top of a hill, we saw a man sitting on a stool. I guessed right away that it must be Thomas Cole, the painter. When I told Tamara, she pretended to know who Thomas Cole is, but I know she didn't really know. Thomas Cole had an easel he was using to paint on, and he was looking out over the river, painting it. I wonder if our house will be in his painting.

I don't know that I could teach the students to write journal entries in response to, or in alignment with, each other, the way Tamara and Felicia do. Their writing demonstrates the consequences of a social aesthetic experience. Witnessing these girls rehearse and then write these journal entries, I see that when they look at the painting, Tamara really does think the figure might have a weapon, and Felicia knows immediately that it must be the painter, and she produces the artist's name with great aplomb. So the girls incorporate elements of their aesthetic interactions, and their personal interactions, into the narratives of their journals. It is rather a fascinating transaction, and it makes me wonder how much autobiography there is in all the children's writing. Felicia and Tamara are not the only students to refer to each other's writing in their own entries. There is something about the social environment of engaging together with the painting that introduces social processes into their writing. From the entries written around this painting, we end up with almost a village record.

This social process, combined with writing that starts with looking, brings into the writing community some students who have yet to complete a piece in writing workshop and gives me the opportunity to make new discoveries about students who are not easy to know in the classroom. Which brings us to Justin.

Justin doesn't like to read, and he has never written more than a sentence or two in class. He has been in four fifth grades in two years and has been living in a homeless shelter recently. Justin spends a long time looking at the painting and posing questions about what he sees. Then he listens to some other students' entries. Here is an excerpt from his journal entry:

> I am where there is thunder and lots of dangerous animals and I hear the animals and rain. There is a light part where there are fields and sunshine and quiet but it is behind me and it feels like I can never be there. It's like I am always alone and it is always dark. Other people live in the light part. I ran up to the dark dangerous part today because I didn't like how my family acts around their friends and how they treat me different.
>
> Well, I'm in the dangerous part now. I see a dirty pond full of shadows and rotting leaves, and a sudden cliff hidden behind trees and wet bushes and also a big storm coming towards me. So I run so the tornado or storm doesn't take me off my feet. I hide in a burnt out tree that has been hit by lightning. It's dark in the tree, but it's a different kind of dark, not a scarey [sic] dark but a warm dark. I tell myself that my family might be worried about me and they might be looking for me. So, I leave this dark, this tree, and I go home and when I go home everybody hangs around me like I've been gone for a week. So, I tell my mother why I ran away and she tells me that she didn't know how I felt. She tells me that she is sorry and that everything will be back to normal, only better

Justin shows that he is setting his entry in the landscape of the painting. For me, though, it is more important to see how, by engaging with the painting, Justin finds a way to express his own sentiments in his writing. In fact, transporting himself into an alternative, imagined setting seems to help him find the freedom to describe in writing some of how he feels about his lived experience. When Justin shares his piece with the class, we discover that he has thoughts about the light and the dark and that he has poetic leanings toward metaphor. We see that he tries to express what a boy who wants everything to stay safe feels, and what it is like when that safety is threatened. We see that by placing his narrator in the painting, Justin has been able to illustrate how a boy who is treated differently feels, and how that boy finds a way to reach out to his family. We feel a little closer to Justin, and he seems to feel closer to us and to the class. When he shares his piece, another boy in the class who also lives in a shelter says that he will run away too in his piece, and he can come upon Justin in the hollow tree, and they can be safe in the warm dark together, and they will never actually leave the painting, unless it is to visit another one. They go off together to find another painting to inhabit. This is what I mean by an aesthetic experience. Justin finds new ways to describe his emotional landscape through his participation with this painted landscape.

ASSUMING A ROLE IN A HISTORY PAINTING

Justin starts to discover his voice as a writer when he engages with painting in order to write. Other students may discover voices that have been historically overwritten or overlooked, or with which they simply do not feel sympathetic. The social studies or humanities classroom is a natural place for this kind of writing experience, because so much of the work we do there is about reconstructing history in order to learn more about ourselves. This kind of research is informed by empathy and is geared toward possibility. I have also found that the writing students do when they engage with moments of historical consequence may interrupt writing processes that are becoming stagnant for them. Sometimes a student seems to get stuck in writing poetry, or personal narrative, or long stories, all of them showing absorption only with the self. So the writing I describe here takes place in social studies or humanities classrooms because that is where we initiated it, but its consequences expand beyond these disciplines. It is writing that looks out, that looks beyond our own concerns.

American history paintings, those paintings that record critical historical events or scenes, are particularly effective at stimulating critical and empathetic responses. Following the European tradition of glorifying the exploits of monarchs and generals, these paintings traditionally record real or invented moments in history. Part of this tradition is the actual creation of critical moments, so that events that may have been bloody and random come to seem organized and heroic. When we look at American history paintings with children, we are looking at both artistic interpretations and propaganda. These paintings demonstrate that history *is* interpretation. Writing from within an artistic rendering thus asks children to place themselves within a certain historical moment and within a certain historical perspective. We could do the same thing with primary source texts, but more and more I am realizing that the primary source documents, especially those we so often bring to elementary and middle school social studies classrooms, are not at appropriate literacy levels for children. They were not written for children, they are not the most effective texts for teaching strategies for reading comprehension, and the students gain only the most partial understanding of the meaning of the documents.

This thinking is leading me more and more to consider the visual images and other historical and artistic artifacts with which we can reconstruct a sense of

FIGURE 2–5   *Prisoners from the Front,* Homer

American experiences. Eisner writes that "through music, painting, poetry, and story, we can participate in worlds that otherwise would be closed to us" (1994, 17). I have found there is something especially compelling about history paintings, the way they pull us back to the past so that we participate in history. In a study of the Civil War experience, for instance, I particularly like Homer's paintings, because he pulls us right into intimate moments. Homer sketched and painted many of these images as an illustrator for *Harper's Weekly* during the war years, and they were printed in that and other journals. *Prisoners from the Front*, Homer's 1866 painting in the Metropolitan, for example, shows a Yankee officer guarding Confederate prisoners (see Figure 2–5 and go to *www.heinemann.com/ehrenworth*).

Homer is clearly presenting a Northern perspective. The Yankee officer is dapper and upright, not even needing the long sword at his side to subdue his prisoners. He wears a gentleman's riding hat atop his head, and his high leather boots are polished and supple. His aide's rifle glitters. The eyes of all men are on this officer. The Confederates, in contrast, wear uniforms that are unbuttoned, and their rifles are thrown to the ground in submission. And yet, the artist seems also to imply respect for these Southern soldiers. They stand tall, and their expressions are not boorish, but rather curious, as if they wonder, calmly, about their fate now. Knowing what we know about prisoner of war camps in the Civil War, and about the conditions of the prison ships in New York Harbor and Andersonville, we may pity these men more than did Homer. Homer brings us back, but we bring our own knowledge with us. The dark colors of the image blend into a dusty scene of dirt, wrecked fields, and masculine order.

When I look at a painting for the first time with students, I describe it aloud the way I just did here. What I am doing is looking closely and describing what I see, and I am imagining the implications of these observations. This process may feel awkward at first if you haven't often spoken aloud of art, but it soon becomes natural. You are reading the painting. You are demonstrating an aesthetic engagement. You are speaking aloud the things you may choose to write.

Taking the Paintings as Landscapes for Our Writing

FIGURE 2–6 *Prisoners from the Front,* Homer (detail)

I ask students who are studying American history to imagine the perspective of someone who is in the scene of a history painting. It is open genre. Some of the students write invented letters, others write bulletins from the front and dispatches. Others write journal entries, and some simply write vignettes. Warren, an eighth grader, looks at Homer's *Prisoners from the Front* (see Figure 2–6) and writes:

He looked at the Yankee soldier standing in front of him, and he automatically reached to button and smooth his uniform. But some of the buttons had been torn off in yesterday's battle. So he pushed his cap a little forward on his head, and straightened his shoulders. He slouched just a little, to show that he was not afraid. He ignored the man with the gun, and looked directly at the Yankee officer, wondering if the man knew how to use the sword.

Warren takes the perspective of the Confederate officer. In social studies, because of students' outrage over the conditions of slavery, it has been almost impossible for any of the students to articulate this perspective. The painting, a painting created by a Northern artist, depicting a Northern triumph, nevertheless stirs in Warren a kind of empathy, so that he imagines the reactions of this Confederate, the kind of pride, and even arrogance, that he retains even in defeat. Warren begins with looking, which is how he discovers this imagined moment and the words to describe it. It is a more detailed, a more empathetic, and a more suggestive piece of writing than he has yet created for social studies or for language arts. I hope this may help Warren learn to use details in order to suggest attitude and atmosphere in his essay and fiction writing. Clearly he can do it. Consider the phrase "wondering if the man knew how to use the sword." It is rife with suggestions of mockery and pride. There is a quality of the implicit. You can see how we can help the students make suggestions in their writing by seeking the suggestive implications of the images. It is a way of learning to notice, to read, to think, and to write.

Creating the Possibility of Alternative Perspectives and Lost Voices

One concern I have when we look at any images or texts that record the American experience is how we acknowledge the many voices and perspectives that have been overwritten and lost in the making and recording of American history. It is preferable not to start with the master narrative of white settlement, but instead to begin with the histories of those people who were originally on the land, and then perhaps to move to those people who were brought here by force. These narratives would then serve to interrupt the settlement narratives of colonialism and manifest destiny. When I think about ways to initiate writing through the visual arts, therefore, I turn to history paintings that have unexpected characters in them or try to look through the master narratives that inform the paintings.

Children may be adept at seeking out alternate narratives. Spencer, for instance, looks at the much-reproduced *Washington Crossing the Delaware* by Emanuel Leutze, 1851 (Figure 2–7). The painting shows General Washington, in profile, crossing over the icy Delaware River. He stands proudly in the prow of the

FIGURE 2–7   Washington Crossing the Delaware, Leutze

FIGURE 2–7   *Washington Crossing the Delaware,*
Leutze (detail)

boat, looking forward resolutely as his men pull at oars and pole the ice, while the flag billows behind him in a sweeping upward arc. It is a heroic scene that has less to do with real historical events than with the making of historical memory. The painting won such acclaim with the American people and government that the artist had to make a second version and finally a third version for engraving.

When the students are choosing history paintings to write from, Spencer points out in class the figure of a black man in the prow of the boat, pulling at an oar (see Figure 2–8). Spencer immediately chooses to write from the perspective of this figure. He creates a narrative describing how this man was originally a river man who ferried people across icy rivers in winter. According to Spencer's narrative, because of his skill, this river man joined General Washington's boat, the first one to cross the river, and he helped to get it safely to the other side.

Spencer then decides to invent this figure as one of his own ancestors, and he makes his journal a "found" one that has been discovered in an attic. While he is writing, Spencer says frankly that he never wants to assume a perspective other than a black one, because it just doesn't feel right to him as a black student to pretend to be someone else. Part of my job as Spencer's teacher, therefore, becomes searching out marginalized historical documents that offer other perspectives than those included in what Spencer has helped me see as a dominant curriculum. We start to look at folk art and migration art, for instance, as well as journals and narratives.

When she sees what Spencer is doing, another student returns to Bierstadt's 1863 painting titled *The Rocky Mountains, Lander's Peak* (see Figure 2–9 and go to *www.heinemann.com/ehrenworth*) and writes from the perspective of the Shoshone tribe Bierstadt painted in their mountain hideaway in what is now Wyoming. Claire decides that this painting qualifies as a history painting and not only as a landscape because it documents a moment in history that would soon change. She looks at the painting and writes:

> I talked to the man who is making all the drawings today. He was surprised to hear me speak his language, and to see that I could write. I told him about the years I spent as a servant to Farmer Brown, before I was rescued in a raid. Farmer Brown hurt his hand in the apple press, so he taught me to write so that I could write letters back East asking for supplies. The man is making pictures of our things and the people, but mostly of the land. I know that when the white men see these pictures, they will want to take the land. Farmer Brown showed me how the White man takes

FIGURE 2–9   The Rocky Mountains, Lander's Peak, Bierstadt

anything he wants, and gives only blows in return. You can see this wanting even in this man's picture, how the land is so big, and we become so small, and the light does not reach us.

Claire is doing so many good things here as a writer, things I have never seen her do before, especially in writing that is not personal narrative. She is alternating long sentences with powerful fragments. She is moving from past tense to present tense in a deliberate shift of tone. And she is imagining history. Claire imagines the implications of this white man's fascination with the land, and she offers the perspective of one who will soon be driven from this place. It is always difficult to decide how to write from the perspective of historical peoples who have traditions other than written literacy for their storytelling and record keeping. Claire solves this problem by inserting an anecdote about her time as a captive of a white farmer. The way she describes Farmer Brown is curiously convincing, as is the way she interprets how the artist has emphasized the grandeur of the land over the smallness of the Native Americans. Claire is a writer who tends to write big—long, heavily descriptive stories and personal narratives. Here, I am able to help her to write small—to discipline her writing by limiting her entry to half a page, but to say something with big implications. We see her move toward writing that matters.

THE AESTHETIC EXPERIENCE AND THE TEACHING OF WRITING

One thing that links all of the writing described in this chapter is that it is the consequence of an aesthetic experience. There is something indefinable, something nebulous, and yet something enormously vigorous about the aesthetic experience. Miranda, Willie, Justin, Claire—these students all write with unexpected integrity. Their writing demonstrates complexity in how it weaves the autobiographical with historical interpretation. Artists interpret history, and perhaps that is why artwork demands that we also fulfill our role as interpreters. And yet when we bring ourselves to the art, the element of self-discovery is never absent. Miranda demonstrates this process when she brings her gender concerns to her interpretation of *Cider Making*. She is "working from within," as curriculum theorist William Pinar names the art of interpreting text autobiographically (1992, 9). This kind of engagement is not a passive experience, for the passive experience is one that simply does not exist. Something happens to us when we engage with art. We enter into an implicit compact if not with the artist, then with the work of the artist. It might be that the bravery it takes to simply make a work of art becomes ours, a bit, when we engage the artwork, so that we too try new things and step out into the world, and it is this daring that reveals itself in our writing.

REFERENCES

Allen, C. 2001. *The Multigenre Research Paper: Voice, Passion, and Discovery in Grades 4–6*. Portsmouth, NH: Heinemann.

Ambrose, S. 1996. *Undaunted Courage*. New York: Simon & Schuster.

Dewey, J. 1900/1990. *The School and Society*. Chicago: University of Chicago Press.

Eisner, W. 1994. *Cognition and Curriculum Reconsidered*. New York: Teachers College Press.

Pinar, W. 1992. *Autobiography, Politics and Sexuality*. New York: Peter Lang.

Rodriguez Roque, O. 1987. *The United States of America*. New York: Metropolitan Museum of Art.

Romano, T. 2000. *Blending Genre, Altering Style: Writing Multigenre Papers*. Portsmouth, NH: Heinemann.

Books with American Landscape and History Paintings

Driscoll, J. 1997. *All That Is Glorious Around Us: Paintings from the Hudson River School*. Ithaca, NY: Cornell University Press.

Minks, L. 2000. *The Hudson River School: The Landscape Art of Bierstadt, Cole, Church, Durand, Heade, and Twenty Others*. New York: Barnes and Noble.

Rodriguez Roque, O. 1987. *The United States of America*. New York: Metropolitan Museum of Art.

Wilton, A. 2002. *American Sublime: Landscape Painting in the United States 1820–1880*. Princeton, NJ: Princeton University Press.

Historical Journals, Diaries, Memoirs and Fiction

Gregory, K. 1996. *Across the Wide and Lonesome Prairie: The Oregon Trail Diary of Hattie Campbell, 1847*. Dear America Series. New York: Scholastic.

Heath, D. ed. 1986. *Mourt's Relation: A Journal of the Pilgrims at Plymouth*. Bedford, MA: Applewood.

www.isu.edu/~trinmich/Oregontrail.html   Website with maps, authentic diary excerpts, and information about the Oregon Trail.

www.ukans.edu/kansas/seneca/oregon/mainpage.html Site with diaries, including excerpts from the logs of the Donner Party.

Websites with Images of American Paintings

www.metmuseum.org   This website allows you to access the museum's collection. Enter and click on "American painting and sculpture," and you will find all the images in this chapter and many other lovely landscapes and history paintings, which you can view on your computer or download and print. You can also access the Met Store at this website, where you can purchase cards and posters of American landscapes.

www.worcesterart.org/Collection/american2.html   The American Painting collection of the Worcester Art Museum.

http://xroads.virginia.edu   The American studies department of the University of Virginia. Many images and lots of information about the American experience over the last three hundred years.

http://xroads.virginia.edu/~CAP/NATURE/cap3.html   Website from the American studies department of the University of Virginia, which has information about and images of Thomas Moran's paintings of the West, especially the Rockies and the great canyons.

Chapter Three

Telling Stories of the World

Short Story Writing and Flexible Cultural Perspectives

It is most important to know about lives that seem, on the surface, unlike our own.
—Naomi Shihab Nye

Sometimes I want to see my students lifted out of their private absorptions, to have them see how many ways there are to engage with the world and how many ways there are to tell the story of being in the world. I want us to try to understand each other across vast disconnects of experience. The world is a big place, and we have many things to understand about each other if we are not to stand tragically in opposition. I want children to see their story in others' stories and to seek ways to understand each other with sympathy and grace and humor. I want them to see what it feels like to abandon the ways of knowing that we inherit. I want them to cultivate flexible perspectives. This takes practice. It is hard to imagine perspectives other than our own. It is probably only when we are still young that most of us are open to developing sympathetic, flexible perspectives.

We can lure children into practicing flexible perspectives by writing short stories that are set not in our own culture but in another. We can help them make these stories culturally informed by showing children how to incorporate cultural artifacts within the story. The task involves inquiry, observation, and imagination, qualities that I can't help but feel are generative of good in the world. And so this chapter describes ways to teach children to write short stories that shift the perspective of the writer and the reader culturally, stories that blend modern American short story elements with those of folktale and fable, stories that begin with looking at artifacts and ultimately imagine many ways to be in the world.

DEVELOPING SYMPATHETIC PERSPECTIVES IN SCHOOL

So much of the world now seems animated by a spirit of fear and hatred. It seems constitutive of the state of incipient hostility that pervades this nation and others. And I wonder, for instance, if it would make a difference if we adults had to imagine stories set in all the places we set bombs. What would it mean to imagine a young mother in Afghanistan, a little girl in Nagasaki, a boy, now, in Iraq? Would our imaginations stretch across national borders and identities? The English poet Sassoon, fighting at the front for almost all of the First World War, used to send poems back to the home press so that those who condoned war but did not actually have to kill, or bear the loneliness and fear of death and mutilation, would still have to bear witness. In 1917 Sassoon sent home a poem titled "To the Warmongers," part of which reads:

> I'm back again from hell
> With loathsome thoughts to sell;
> Secrets of death to tell;
> And horrors from the abyss.
> Young faces smeared with blood,
> Sucked down into the mud (Hart-Davis 1994, 77)

In the almost five years he spent in active duty, Sassoon came to envision the German soldiers at the front, and their mothers at home, knitting caps and socks, as no different from himself, and he described how he *lost the urge to keep killing*. Sassoon returned, always to the front, because he would not abandon his comrades to die alone in the trenches. He asked the world, however, to bear witness to the realities of war. His poems are a paean to human loss, and suffering, and atrocities witnessed and remembered. They work to eliminate the distance between what we can condone and what we can bear.

As we balanced on the brink of another world war in 1934, philosopher John Dewey remarked that

> unless the schools of the world can engage in a common effort to rebuild the spirit of common understanding, of mutual sympathy and goodwill among all peoples and races, to exorcise the demons of prejudice, isolation and hatred, the schools themselves are likely to be submerged by the general return to barbarism, which is the sure outcome of present tendencies if they go unchecked by the forces which education alone can evoke and fortify. (1934, 14)

It is hard to feel that we are not still in that place, and that part of the work of schooling *must* be the development of sympathetic outlooks. What do we do with these concerns, though, as teachers? We are not going to read Sassoon with elementary and middle school children, nor are we going to bring the specter of war and hatred into classrooms. But are there ways in the teaching of writing that we can come to care a bit for the world?

WRITING AS A MEANS OF PRACTICING FLEXIBLE PERSPECTIVES

When I think about writing that engages with the world, I think of Shelley Harwayne's ideas about writing that enriches our community, including writing for what she calls real-life purposes (2001). I think also of Randy and Katherine Bomer's work and how they encourage teachers and children to construct writing around social action and ideas of social justice (2001). And there are other ways, also, to write so that we think more of others and less of ourselves, less explicit ways that ask us to engage creatively and sympathetically with other cultures and other ways of being in the world. Stories are one way that we come to know in empathetic ways experiences and outlooks with which we are unfamiliar. If we ask our students to actually imagine themselves into another culture, to write that perspective into existence in a short story, we activate a spirit of sympathetic imagination and inquiry. I hope that this experience implicitly lessens the very notion of *the other*, so that we can realign ourselves in more humane ways with notions of *we*.

We can scaffold these processes by constructing stories around cultural artifacts so that children actively engage with another culture in a way that makes it seem real. Asking the students to use cultural artifacts in their stories also helps them structure their stories. They have some specific *things*, some objects that they need to describe and incorporate contextually. This concrete task helps young writers. Fiction is hard. Working with story structures and inventing narratives and characters are not easy tasks for young writers, so that often the work we do in writing short or realistic or historical fiction does not really make them better writers; we do it because they become better readers. When we explore cultural artifacts, however, the children do not have to invent *everything*. The details come from what they see. Some of the narrative is generated around what they come to know about these artifacts. It is a rigorous imagination that we are asking them to develop, one that is purposeful and directed and informed by real objects made by human hands.

I describe here how to focus short story writing on the culture and royal artifacts of the kingdom of Benin in Nigeria. Children write short stories set within Benin, and their stories incorporate a number of cultural artifacts. You may choose to approach another culture. You may choose to approach the Inuit or the Iroquois or the Ashanti. You can imagine that the structures that support this way of writing will remain the same, but the children will look at different artifacts and will build different cultural knowledge that will inform their stories. Or you may initiate the study I describe as an interactive model, and the students may then independently explore various cultures. I usually teach this unit as a class-room inquiry because when the students are pursuing independent inquiries, it can be hard to know enough to support them well, and I find myself looking more at content than at how they write, or I am caught up myself in making meaning of the content. But there is something lovely also about the idea of locating our collective imaginations in many places around the world.

I have in the past opened up the genre choice in this workshop so that students have more choice. It would be easy to write informational pamphlets, or museum guides, or nonfiction articles around the artifacts. Eventually, however, I find myself returning to stories, because it is in the art of creating a story that we have to demonstrate sympathetic understanding. An informational pamphlet simply does not demand the same act of sympathetic imagination. I want the writing to be an artistic act. I want the students to demonstrate not simply new knowledge, but new *perspectives*.

WHY BENIN? IMPLICATIONS AND UNDERSTANDINGS

I describe how we engage the artifacts of Benin here really to demonstrate how to engage with any artifacts in order to write short stories in this particular way. The decision for my own class to focus on Benin, however, reflects several inter-related concerns. These include concerns about how race and ethnicity are con-structed as oppressive narratives outside of school and inside. The narratives that we explore in school are often dominant Western ones, or ones that filter other experiences through this same dominant perspective. There must be times that curriculum itself feels oppressive, and some students resist it, and this may be just one of the many reasons schooling is a more congenial and successful place for affluent white children than other children. How would it be different if we studied the Harlem Renaissance as the epitome of the black experience, rather than slave narratives? Would it engender feelings of disruption and liberation? What would it mean to say that our curriculum is going to be one of disruption, as bell hooks advocates in *Teaching to Transgress* (1994)? Would it mean the possi-bility of changed outlooks and flexible perspectives?

So in looking toward Benin, I have some curricular desires. I want to offer counternarratives to some of the master narratives offered in the curriculum. I want to look closely at objects that exert cultural affect. I am eager to look at how the traditions of other cultures unsettle the notions of religion and government we have learned through our predominantly Western curriculum, notions that have come to seem commonsense. I am also drawn by particular objects that en-hance the positions of women as positions of power. And the art historian in me wants objects of great beauty.

And so we could have come elsewhere, but for now, for this study, we come to Benin. The concepts about Benin that undergird this study are grounded in Ezra's

The Royal Art of Benin: The Perls Collection, which was published by the Metropolitan Museum of Art in 1992. It is a comprehensive guide to the art and culture of Benin, with some maps, some photographs of the modern Oba and Iyoba in ceremonial dress, and many gorgeous reproductions of sculptures and artifacts. In the Appendix (see pages 144–46), I have tried to summarize some of the information in this text more thoroughly than I do in this chapter.

This text describes Benin as a medieval kingdom and a modern republic within the state of Nigeria. The ruler is known as the *Oba* (see Figure 3–1). He seems to be responsible for the prosperity and health of the people, and he is thought to wield powers greater than the natural on behalf of his people. His mother, the *Iyoba,* also wields great powers. Religious and political acts seem tightly interwoven. The royal art objects of Benin are ones of great beauty, to which great meaning is attached. They are ceremonial objects used for grave purposes having to do with the well-being of the kingdom. The Oba may pray to cast brass altar heads of his ancestors in times of trouble. Altar bells may alert ancestor spirits, and rattle staffs may call benevolent spirits. Many of these ritual objects are in the process of being returned to Nigeria now, as cultural leaders in Nigeria negotiate with the British Museum and other collections. In this age of modern reproductions, we will not lose all contact with the objects when they do return to their natural place of origin. They may bring us with them, shift our attention to other realms, other peoples and places and ways of living.

The ceremonial objects of Benin are sacred and splendid. In terms of objects that help children write, they are effective not only for their sheer magnificence but also because they have certain ceremonial purposes that we can reiterate in our stories. Also, the carving is detailed and clear, and there are a variety of related objects, all of them sharing certain pictorial language and symbolism. So in considering the royal art of Benin, put simply, there is a lot to work from to build a knowledge base with which to construct historically informed stories. And in valuing these objects in our stories, we inevitably practice shifting our perspective.

The children may not come to know Benin in the sense of knowing fully and

FIGURE 3–1   Head of an Oba (detail)

accurately, if that is ever possible in historical inquiries. But we hope that they may come to know sympathetically. And we can embrace that sense of ambiguity as a way to retain complexity and uncertainty in curriculum. As Eisner puts it, that ambiguity "has its cognitive virtues. A school culture that fosters the quest for certainty encourages dispositions antithetical to the intellectual life." He adds that "intellectual life is characterized by the absence of certainty, by the inclination to see things from more than one angle, by the thrill of the search more than the closure of the find" (1994, 71). I think of the children's work as approaching this culture. We are approaching understanding. Our work is not to locate the "right" ideas. Our work is to write into existence new ways of thinking and being in the world.

It can be helpful to see if there are literary as well as artistic traditions that can inform our inquiry and our writing. Benin has a rich tradition of legends and folktales. These stories have been told in some form orally for perhaps hundreds of years and have been written down in English pretty recently. Many of the stories take the form of "how something came to be," like so many of the Greek myths. Others of them are cautionary tales intended to regulate human behavior. There is more humor in them, though, than in the Greek myths—more of a generous spirit, a warmth, and an acceptance of human failure. My favorite collection is *Why Goats Smell Bad and Other Stories from Benin* by Raouf (1998), because the stories are short and lucid. So if we follow some of the storytelling traditions that exist in Benin, we can work to be concise and purposeful in our writing.

WHY SHORT STORIES?

All teachers who have taught short stories or any kind of fiction writing with children know that it can be a train wreck. There is a reason that literary scholars consider short story writing to be perhaps the greatest contribution American writers have made to literature. It is one of the most challenging of all writing genres. Every word matters. Meaning must happen quickly. As readers, we are able to keep it all in our heads at one time, so that we see the whole arc of the story and all the parts at once, even as we move through it. There is great potential for complexity, implicit meaning, and ambiguity, and yet these happen within a trajectory that is brief. Literary theorist Eve Sedgwick remarks on the way that fiction readers make an inexplicit compact with the author, so that, as she puts it, they "voluntarily plunge into worlds that strip them, however temporarily, of the painfully acquired cognitive maps of their ordinary lives" (1990, 97). Reading short stories can be a mesmerizing and a brutal experience because it is so quickly ended.

All of this means that short stories are powerful stuff. It feels intimidating, even a little foolhardy, to explore this genre with children. And yet it has the potential to be a heady experience. There is so much to teach that may help the children as writers. Creating structure. Developing an idea purposefully. Developing characters and settings swiftly. Demonstrating or suggesting change. Writing implicitly. Writing concisely. Creating movement through time and place and emotional spaces. Often this is just too much to teach within one unit, and it is too hard to jettison much of the teaching and still be writing short stories. The danger is that we either end up working on our stories for ridiculous amounts of time, or the stories just fall apart, and it is not clear at the end of the unit if the children are better writers. They almost always become better readers. They begin to notice story structure. They may notice leads and shifts and resolutions. They talk knowledgeably about the need for the reader to make inferences. They can better trace what an author is doing. But it is a lot of writing time to occupy if the children don't emerge as stronger writers as well as better readers.

Our work as short story writers in this project is actually easier because we have certain clear parameters. It is these boundaries that make the project accessible. These factors include that the story be purposeful in some way, akin to the folktales and legends of Benin. These stories explain how something came to exist or be the way it is in Benin, or instruct us in moral behavior, or describe the consequences of human actions. So our short story may teach the reader something. For instance, Raouf tells the story of the unwanted child. A king abandons a child who is ugly to look at. The child grows up to save the kingdom with his courage. The king *and the reader* learn that we should not judge humans by their appearances, we should wait to judge them by their actions.

This kind of purposeful structure is accessible to even very young writers. Third grader Willie, for instance, explains how the first altar is made, and why it is made of mud. His story reads:

The Mud Altar

> Long ago in Africa, in West Africa, there was a boy who was born in a muddy village. He was poor. His family was poor. He had a sister and she was poor and muddy. They were muddy all the time. They lived in small huts and the mud came inside. It got in their clothes and their food. No-one knew what to do with so much mud.
>
> One day, the Oba visited the village. He was king of all Benin. He wore necklaces around his neck of orange beads. He had scars on his forehead to show he was brave. His hair was in long braids to show he was strong. Oba stayed the night in the village and the village put him in a hut. He got very muddy.
>
> Oba wanted to pray to his father, who was dead and was now a god-spirit. He had the brass head so he could speak to his father. He had the tusk that showed his father as Oba. But he had nowhere to put them. He put them down in the mud and cried.

The boy was outside the hut sitting in the mud. He heard Oba cry and he came inside. He asked Oba what was wrong. Oba said "I don't have anywhere to put the head of my father." The boy said "I will help you." He sat in the mud and he made a table out of the mud. The Oba put his father's head on the table and he was happy.

This is a story about why the altars in Benin are made out of mud. And it also shows how we should make the best of things.

Willie's story follows the traditions of Benin folktales closely. It is brief. It has clear practical and moral implications. Struggling writers benefit from structure like this that is almost a template. But Willie is also working on character and setting and how they are interrelated in ways that create tension. The Oba and the boy are united by the mud. It brings the palace dweller and the villager together in a problematic situation.

Willie also incorporates the artifacts he has looked at. I ask the children to include some of the artifacts they study in their writing. I ask this of them for two reasons. One is that this task demands that they engage closely with the artifacts and thus with cultural beliefs and traditions. The children work with images of real objects. They may not simply make stuff up about this culture. They may suggest, but they must back up their ideas with detailed observation and interpretation. This is good practice for all writing. The second reason I ask them to include artifacts is that it helps them ground their stories in the culture they are studying. It gives them a way to incorporate what they observe and learn, it keeps their stories historically informed, but most importantly, it asks them to imagine a perspective that values these objects. Willie's story convinces. Likewise, ninth grader Julia writes in her story that

> the young Oba knelt before the mud altar to pray. He prayed for rain so that his people would have food to eat. He prayed for wisdom and for power, power over the clouds and the air. He looked into the eyes of the altar head of his great-grandfather and he felt himself looking through those eyes. He was no longer only a boy who had become king too early. He was a great Oba who could direct the winds and the skies to bring rain for his people. He called on the clouds to come down from the mountains. He heard them answer and he heard, in his mind, the sound the wet droplets made, falling already on the villages.

When the children describe the Oba praying to the altar head of an ancestor, they shift, a little, into his territory. In demonstrating that this action makes sense within their stories, in making it real for their reader, they show that there are many ways to inhabit the world. They give up, a little, the sense of opposition that places us apart and against each other.

FINDING AND READING THE IMAGES

The artifacts are the lure, and the mystery, and they are didactic in their mystery—they can pull the children in and teach them in this study. In *Art Works!* Dana Balick explains how she learned to "read" an Iroquois sweet grass basket as a "way to enter into the Iroquois culture" (Balick and Wolf 1999, 156). In the same way, before we look at any secondary sources, I look at the sculptures and objects with the children. We look closely, we make observations, we wonder about their purpose and nature. It may be a dislocating experience for some children who have not looked at non-Western art or cultural traditions before. It is liberating for others. I share my ideas with the children about developing flexible perspectives, about imagining other ways of thinking, as well as about learning to observe, and interpret, and suggest in our writing. I share my concerns that our world is becoming a place where it is easier to strike back than to reach across. I explain that I want us to open our imaginations to these images, to let them reposition us so that we may shift others.

To find images for the cultures you choose to approach, look in the library, in museum bookstores, and on the Internet. Ask for help from institutions. If we were going to look at the Iroquois, for instance, I would probably first call the Museum of the American Indian and ask for help. Curators and museum educators and librarians share our work. And we need their help, because the textbooks and nonfiction books we have in schools are neither gorgeous nor constructive. So when looking for material on the Inuit, for instance, I would go to *www.yahoo.com* and enter "Inuit." I would find the Inuit Art Foundation, and I would email or call to ask for posters and book loans and recommendations for other resources.

If you choose to follow this Benin study, you can visit the companion website *(www.heinemann.com/ehrenworth)* for more information on the sources I mention here. The two books that I have found most helpful because they have so many large-scale, detailed reproductions of royal ceremonial objects and sculptures are *The Pacific Islands, Africa and the Americas* (1987) and *The Royal Art of Benin: The Perls Collection* (1992), both published by the Metropolitan Museum. You might want to ask your library to get either of these on loan, and then you will have access to all the images. I make copies and put them in plastic slipcovers, and the children work from these reproductions. I make multiple copies of the Oba (the king), the Iyoba (queen mother), an altar tusk, an altar bell, a rattle staff, and a neck ring, so that the students can choose among these objects as ones to incorporate in their stories. All these images are here for you and on the companion website. It is also helpful to try to enlarge details of the images so that the children can really look closely. The hand at the top of the rattle staff is holding a mudfish, the symbol of good fortune. The neck ring is decorated with vultures picking at the decapitated heads of victims. Close-up enlargements let the children notice and incorporate such detail in their work.

FIGURE 3–2   *Iyoba* (detail)

We can give the children some context for the objects by describing what cultural historians and curators say about their history. I tell the children a little about what we know about this culture, and the significance of these objects, at least as represented in this case by these museum catalogs. I start with what seems most important. So in creating a context for the royal art of Benin, I introduce the idea that the country is cared for by the *Oba*, or king. Holding up the image of the Oba, I explain that the brass altar heads of the Obas were believed to allow the Oba to speak to his ancestors, and that they were placed on mud altars. This is a significant concept—that these are sacred objects through which humans communicated with spirits. I note that the heads of the Obas are marked by cultural symbols of beauty and strength, including high cheekbones, wide, heavily outlined eyes, ritual scars above the brow, braided sidelocks, and rows of coral bead necklaces. The Oba also usually wears a small round cap as a symbol of his rank. In the center of the cap is a hole, and into this is placed the altar tusk, which is carved with symbols of the Oba's many accomplishments.

I am trying to give the children both some context and some expectation of what they are going to see when they begin to look closely at the objects. A sense of familiarity helps them engage with the objects intimately. So holding up an image of the Iyoba, or queen mother, I describe how the altar heads of the Iyobas served a similar purpose as those of the Obas and are also marked by bead necklaces and scarification (see Figure 3–2). The Iyoba's hair is dressed in a high conical design. I say that other objects of ritual importance are the altar bells and rattle staffs, which are used to alert spirits and ancestors. These may be carved with ritual designs or signs of good fortune, such as the mudfish. There are also altar rings, thought perhaps to be worn by sacrificial victims. They are often carved with figures of prisoners.

Reading a sculpture is like reading a painting, which is like reading a poem. Just look very closely and say aloud for the children what you see. We observe details, and we see connections between sculptures. I read at least one sculpture with the children together before they begin exploring all the objects closely on their own. When I read, I say aloud what I see, and I try to articulate the overall impression first and then note the details that support this impression. If we look at the carved brass altar head of the Iyoba, for instance, I interpret the sculpture as giving an impression of great pride, combined with beauty and strength. I have the impression of pride from how she holds her head so high. I have also read in *The Royal Art of Benin* that the many necklaces are a means to keep the chin always up in this regal posture, and I share this idea with the children. I have the impression of beauty from the high cheekbones and large, heavily outlined eyes and upswept hair. Clearly, attention has been given to appearance. I have an impression of strength from the ritual scars and also from the impassivity of her gaze. She seems remote. It does not feel like a portrait of a woman so much as a depiction of a queen or goddess. I may add that the many coral bead necklaces do seem to hold her head up in a stiff, almost haughty pose, and that her hair seems heavy, so that it also pulls her head backward a bit. The form altogether seems one that sweeps upward. I may note that she has long braids, or sidelocks, similar to the Oba's. If I have one of the museum catalogs in the room, we may notice that most heads of the Iyobas show similar features and symbols, and that there has been very little change to the brass carvings over hundreds of years.

In this lesson I am modeling how to look closely and how to substantiate interpretations of artwork with details from the artwork. Later, I will show the children how to make this same move in their writing. You can also see how we can show that this is the same work we do in interpreting text. We read closely and support interpretations with details from the text. We can bring in ideas and supporting evidence from related sources. I hope that this work here with art demonstrates that this kind of methodology is just that: it is a way of working that is not isolated to an individual lesson or activity.

So I am both modeling interpretation and essentially handing over some established ideas that will give the children places to start. Because this is a cultural inquiry, I am not asking the children to interpret the objects free of all cultural knowledge, but rather in relation to that cultural knowledge. The children then may engage with the images in effective and sympathetic ways.

Figures 3–3 through 3–11 show the images we look at when we are studying the royal art of Benin. The sculptures, with the exception of the rattle staff, which is wood, are all made of carved brass. Their original color is a kind of dark, golden brown. Whatever cultural artifacts you and the children look at, try to make sure that the reproductions are as clear and as large-scale as possible, so that you do justice, as far as possible, to the power of the originals. Also, just as when they work with written text, it is easier for the children to do interpretive work if they do not have to put all their effort into decoding. Large and clear.

FIGURE 3–3   Head of an Oba

FIGURE 3–4   Head of an Iyoba

IMPLEMENTING THE WORKSHOP

Learning Centers: Scaffolding the Inquiry

I think of our work in creating these short stories in two parts. The first part is our study of the cultural artifacts. I usually have reproductions of the objects up on the walls and on our tabletops. As just described, when looking at Benin, I begin by looking at the altar head of an Oba or Iyoba, and I introduce the royal culture of Benin as we examine the sculpture. I am usually with the children in a large-group meeting area for this conversation. Next, I introduce the other objects, not looking in detail at them, but simply telling the children what we know of their purpose so that they have some context in which to understand what they will be looking at. Then I send them off in partnerships or small groups to examine the other objects closely.

Often I organize the images into learning centers. To help the children with the process of observing and interpreting, I give them instructions for each learning center. The instructions help them look closely and also help them *record* their observations in a variety of ways. I suggest that they make some sketches. I suggest that they

FIGURE 3–5   Altar Ring

annotate these drawings. I pose some interpretive questions. All of these devices are aimed at getting them to look and to record. It is to this work that we will turn when we are constructing our stories. I do tell the children that these methods are part of the processes of historical, cultural, and archaeological methods. Archaeologists and cultural anthropologists make drawings, they record observations, they create theories in order to suggest meaning. So that is our work, too.

In making learning centers, look at the images you have available and think of ways to sort them that will help the children create some theories about the implications of what they observe. Middle school children may do this categorization themselves to practice the work of cultural anthropologists and archaeologists. Otherwise, I separate the images into pairs. I put images together that will help the students articulate cultural concepts when they compare and contrast them. This pushes them to observe, interpret, and theorize in natural steps. I set up the work so that the students are working *as* cultural anthropologists or archaeologists, keeping an archive of drawings and notes they will refer to when they are not in the presence of the objects.

Whether the children sort or I sort, I suggest to the students that cultural anthropologists and curators ask if it is helpful to examine some objects together—are some objects perhaps related in their purpose or in their design? For instance, if we examine a head of an Oba and Iyoba together, we may see how they share cultural signs of power and beauty. We can look at an altar tusk and a neck ring together to see how one shows itself as a symbol of power and one as a symbol of subjugation. We may put an altar bell and a rattle staff together because both are used to alert spirits. To make these pairs of images into learning centers, at each table, place a pair of images and a short text, printed very large and perhaps glued to construction paper. These are the children's instructions for the learning center. The instructions have to be concise, clear, and printed very, very large.

At the first table (Learning Center 1), for instance, for an upper elementary or middle school class, I may put images of the altar heads of the Oba and Iyoba (see pages 78 and 79). Both of these images show the wide eyes and cheekbones, the scars over the eyes, the coral bead necklaces, the idealized features. Printed in very large font and glued to construction paper, the text at this table says:

Context

In Benin, the Oba is the king and the Iyoba is the mother of the king.

   Together the Oba and Iyoba care for the kingdom.

   When the Oba and Iyoba seek help, they can pray to their ancestors through these sculptures, which are called altar heads.

   Some altar heads show cultural symbols of power, including coral bead necklaces, scars from ritual scarification, upright posture, a round cap for the Oba, and long braids, or sidelocks.

   Some show symbols of beauty, including high cheekbones, large and outlined eyes, long braids, symmetrical features.

FIGURE 3–6   *Altar Tusk*

Instructions

Please make a detailed sketch of each of these heads on clean white paper.

Label symbols of power and beauty in each drawing. Note which symbols are common to both heads and which seem to be unique.

At the second table (Learning Center 2) I may put the images of an altar ring and an altar tusk (Figures 3–5 and 3–6). The altar tusk has many figures on it, including the Oba, priests, and warriors. The neck ring has decapitated figures with vultures pecking at them. The text may say:

Context

The altar tusk is a carved elephant tusk that is placed in the hole in the center of the altar head of the Oba.

The purpose of the altar tusk is to show the important accomplishments of this Oba. The carvings may also include spirits and priests who help the Oba, as well as enemies he defeats.

The altar rings were possibly worn by sacrificial prisoners or placed on altars. Symbols of defeat, including beheadings and death, are often carved on these neck rings.

Instructions

On two clean pieces of white paper, please make a small sketch of the tusk and the neck ring. Next to each, make a close-up sketch of one or more figures from each and label who you think the figures are and their significance.

Underneath your drawing, please explain in one sentence your theory for the significance of some of the figures on the tusk and the neck ring—why do you think they are included on the tusk or neck ring?

At the third table (Learning Center 3) I may put images of the rattle staff and altar bell (Figures 3–7 and 3–8). The bell seems to have carvings of faces on it and little clappers that would make a musical sound. The rattle staff has a carving of a mudfish with a hand holding it for a handle. The text at that table may say:

FIGURE 3–7   Rattle Staff

Context

Wooden rattle staffs are rung by priests and the Oba to call good spirits.

Brass altar bells in Benin are rung by Obas to alert the spirits of their ancestors to their prayers. The mudfish (a catfish) is a sign of good fortune and prosperity in Benin.

Instructions

On two clean pieces of white paper, please make a sketch of each object.

Label and annotate any design on each image that you think may have religious significance.

Learning centers help the children access content and make something with it. Once the centers are set up, the children take responsibility for their work at each center, and we come together at the end of work time to share the ideas the children construct. The children may organize all of their materials in folders, or they may keep archaeologists' notebooks in which they glue all notes, drawings, and reproductions. I encourage the students to keep a page of this notebook or folder for their own questions and theories and another page for any ideas or sketches they may want to jot down for their stories. In this way, I am trying to help them organize their inquiry, gather ideas and information, maintain complexity in their thinking, and work toward autonomy. I am also orchestrating the work so that it will help the children write. The children start the inquiry with me, but they will write from their own observations and their own aesthetic experiences with these objects.

TELLING SHORT STORIES

Usually when students are involved in learning centers, it helps if they are aware of and working toward the larger project. So I invite them into the short story project before we begin our inquiry work. I may begin teaching short story elements while the students are involved in learning centers. I may read aloud some stories. For Benin, I will read aloud some of the folktales from Raouf's collection. I explain that we are approaching this culture through its arts, coming to know some of the cultural concerns and traditions. The work that lies before us is to create an original short story that is informed by some of these concerns and traditions.

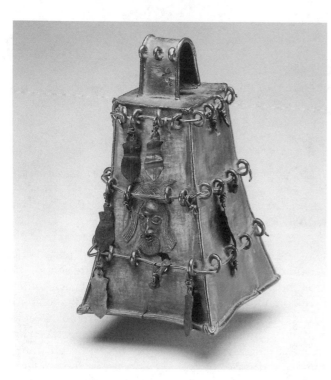

FIGURE 3–8   Altar Bell

After the children have become familiar with the objects, or as they are working, I model the kind of story we will be writing, to demonstrate what I mean by a story that is culturally informed and purposeful, that incorporates some of the artifacts, and that shows a writer trying to shift perspective. We are not writing archaeologists' or anthropologists' reports. We want to write ourselves into other story lines. We are imagining stories other than those we have experienced. I want us to write into existence other narratives, with the hope that the children will retain a sense that our own stories exist in relation to the many story lines at work in the world.

Gathering the children close, I arrange images around me for the children to look at as they listen. Before I start the story, I remind the children of our present tasks as writers. Our stories must be set in Benin. They must be informed by our cultural inquiry. They must weave in artifacts. I ask the children to listen especially for how I include the artifacts. I want the children to notice what I am trying to do so that they can plan their own moves as writers. Because I enjoy oral storytelling and I have become intimate with these artifacts, I often make up stories in the classroom. You may do this, or you may prepare a story ahead of time. Or if you do study Benin, you may retell one I told recently, which appears in the Appendix, on pages 152–54. It begins . . .

Once in a village by a river in Benin twin girls were born five minutes apart and identical in face and body. The girls were known as Elder Sister and Younger Sister. By the time they were twelve the girls wore their hair in dark braids down to their waist. They had bright eyes. They had soft voices. They danced gracefully and when they danced their feet made magic, their voices wove songs, and the beads in their hair rung like bells.

One night the girls were asked to dance for visitors from the palace. In the flickering light of many torches, their feet made intricate patterns in the dust. Their long hair swirled around them, and their voices made soft melodies and

FIGURE 3–9   Altar Ring (detail)   FIGURE 3-10   Altar Tusk (detail)

harmonies against the dark. When Elder Sister and Younger Sister danced, it seemed like the world would always be a place for dancing and for singing and for love. A leopard came from the edge of the jungle to watch. Crocodiles crawled out of the river to listen. Birds stopped their cries so that they could hear the voices of the girls singing. Even the river moved more slowly, pausing to listen to the girls and watch them dance.

After telling the story, I ask the children to notice which artifacts I included in my story and to find them among the images. They may also suggest some purposes of the story, such as to demonstrate how deceit is punished, or to show the relationship between the natural and the human world in Benin, or even to mock human certainty. I deliberately invented a story that demonstrates more than one possible purpose, to maintain complexity. They may notice elements such as the Oba's willingness to resort to sacrifice, or his inability to distinguish between the "bad" sister and the "good," or the way it shows the Oba's relationship to the spirits and nature and how he is responsible for his people. They may question why I make all of Benin suffer when it is the girl who is evil. They may wonder if she is symbolic of the presence of evil, or of our eagerness to name evil.

FIGURE 3–11   Rattle Staff (detail)

Eventually, I ask the children to articulate the aspects of setting, character, tension, and structure in this story, so that they can begin to plan their own stories.

Weaving Story Elements and Structure in Our Stories in Interrelated Ways

There are many different kinds of stories, and there are many ways to start children writing stories. Myths, for instance, often share a common structure related to their purpose of explaining how things came to be or why they are the way they are. So when we write myths, it makes sense to start with structure. A common way to start realistic fiction is with character. Some good short stories, such as many of Hemingway's, revolve around how character is delineated for the reader. And yet other equally powerful short stories, such those by Jorge Luis Borges (1988), don't even really have characters, but offer instead alternate views of realities. The map of the world that is as big as the world. The encyclopedia lost to human knowledge but still influential on human endeavor. It is setting that drives these stories. Borges makes unreal settings seem real immediately. If he has characters at all, they make sense only within that particular setting.

For the stories we are writing, it is the *relationship* between setting and character that is most significant. These stories are a kind of blending of the more oral forms of fables and folktales and the writerly craft of the modern short story. The children's stories need to bring the reader in some way into Benin. Willie's story does that by concentrating on the muddy village. Mine concentrates on the river that runs from the village to the sea. So I ask the children to articulate the setting and then to articulate how their characters are related to that setting. Are they dependent on that setting? Are they trying to break away from or change that setting? Willie's Oba is trying to get rid of all the mud. I have more characters and the setting is more complicated. Younger Sister is trying to escape the village. Oba is trying to bring back the rain. The river separates them and then brings them all together again.

If the children need help with settings, we create a list together of some possibilities, such as a village, the palace, and the jungle. Then the children may do some freewriting around their settings, trying to imagine what is in each setting, including objects and characters. Or they may try to draw their settings and then write from their drawings. Willie's story is unusual in that the setting remains constant and the character changes the setting. Generally it is the characters who move through settings and who change. In mine the setting changes *with* the characters, as the rains disappear and reappear with the acts of the characters. Each of these stories demonstrates some relationship between the setting of the natural world and the humans who inhabit it.

Julia, for instance, wanted to focus her story on how the Oba bears responsibility for his people and that this means he is both accountable for the natural world and yet bound to it and in some way to the supernatural world. So she envisioned a young Oba becoming king in a time of drought. To help her get started, I had her make a simple chart that had the setting on one side and the main character on the other and explained that the two sides had to show some cause and effect or some tension. She had to show the relationship between what she wrote on the left and what she wrote on the right. She filled it in like this:

SETTING	CHARACTER (the Oba)
the palace. Oba dies. Still no rain (altar bells and rattle staffs? ceremonies?)	boy now Oba. Responsible. Afraid to pray. Afraid he is not really a god-spirit but just a boy.
Still no rain. More people die. All Benin asks Oba to intercede for them	Boy can't believe in spirits or in prayer
In palace, at mud altar.	Young oba learns to pray to ancestors. (? Doesn't really believe but does it anyway for his people?)
Rain?	Faith? Miracle? Coincidence? Will he pretend to believe now forever?

You can see that Julia's chart helps her envision how to create tension between the setting and the character, in a way that is peculiarly appropriate to this project. One part of Julia's story reads:

> The young Oba knelt in front of the mud altar and stared at the altar heads. He felt nothing. And while he felt nothing, people died. He felt nothing, and the rains stayed away. He felt nothing, and the clouds passed over Benin to go to other lands. He looked in his heart and he could not find a way to pray when he did not believe. He saw that the altar heads were brass, that they were made by men. He saw that the altar was mud, and that it was made by men. He held out his hand, and it was the hand of a man. It was the hand of a boy.

Julia, a ninth-grade city girl raised Catholic, was herself in the midst of some confusion about religion. She was also a student in a private Catholic school and felt powerless to express these doubts. Julia imagined that it would be possible to have similar confusion even in Benin, even as Oba. She imagined that others, even an Oba, might feel religion as a constraint, and then she imagined what the consequences of those doubts might be in that situation. She imagined that people around this world, in cities and villages, suffer fear and doubt, and she thought about what that might mean. That is cultivating a flexible, sympathetic perspective.

It is not always easy for children to imagine how setting and character can relate in ways that create tension. Sometimes the kind of chart Julia worked on helps. For writers who are struggling to begin, and who also struggle to simply write more, another way to begin is to create outlines and to orally rehearse their stories. If they start this way, it is more helpful to begin with something concrete, like purpose, than to begin with the character-setting relationship. The purposeful fable or folktale structure is an easier one to start with, and then we can turn to character and setting once the students have an outline in place.

I think these decisions are best made not as a class but individually, in side-by-side conversations. Willie, for instance, initially outlined his story about the mud altar by beginning with purpose. His first outline looked like this:

Purpose: how mud altars came to be

> There are no altars in Benin.
> The Oba needs a place to put his ancestors' heads
> A boy builds an altar

Willie had a purposeful structure here. I asked him to look at his outline and rehearse his stories orally with another student, and then to add on to his outline things he found himself saying, especially anything about setting or character or anything that happened. After rehearsing his story with a partner, Willie revised his outline so that it came to look like this:

Purpose: how mud altars came to be

What happens:

> There are no altars in Benin
> But there is a lot of mud
> The Oba needs a place to put his ancestors' heads
> A boy builds an altar out of mud to help the Oba
> Now there are mud altars in Benin

Willie added a final line to his outline that ensured that his story would accomplish his purpose. Mud altars will, indeed, come to be in Benin. I asked him then to look over his drawings and notes of the artifacts and to talk with a partner about which artifacts he would include and how. Willie then expanded his outline to include where he would refer to artifacts, so it looked like this:

Purpose: how mud altars came to be

What happens:

There are no altars in Benin
    altars hold all the heads + objects like bells and stuff
But there is a lot of mud
The Oba needs a place to put his ancestors' heads
    The Oba will wear coral bead necklaces + scars + braids
    the altar head will have a tusk with carvings
A boy builds an altar out of mud to help the Oba
Now there are mud altars in Benin

Next I reminded Willie that he needed to integrate the setting and the characters. Often the children just need to be reminded of what they know in order to make some decisions. So Willie's final outline looked like this:

Purpose: how mud altars came to be
Setting: a village
Narrator: a village boy

What happens:

There are no altars in Benin
    altars hold all the heads + objects like bells and stuff
But there is a lot of mud
The Oba needs a place to put his ancestors' heads the oba will wear coral bead
    necklaces + scars + braids
    the altar head will have a tusk with carvings
A boy builds an altar out of mud to help the Oba
Now there are mud altars in Benin

You can see now how Willie wrote his story from this final outline and also how Willie came to write a story of such length and clear structure. It is really a story of rather extraordinary clarity for a third grader. Willie wrote to meet all the purposes outlined in his structure. Our writing periods, and my efforts in conferring, were spent writing and revising his story so that it met the demands of his outline. Willie's most important revision was the addition of his final line, *And it also shows how we should make the best of things*, which was not in his first draft. This line marked Willie's attempt to make his story a universal one. When he added this line, I saw that he was not only shifting his perspective to Benin but was thinking of a universal audience.

Willie's story works. It is an explicatory tale and also a moral one. A boy helps the Oba, and they learn what to do with all the mud in Benin. Willie's story makes an effective mentor text for young writers, because it is so lucid. I like it, though, because his perspective is convincing. He shows he understands the ritual purpose and the cultural need for these altars. He takes the perspective that is perhaps his own, of a boy who wants to make a difference in the world, a boy who feels powerless. He imagines how such a boy could come to make a difference in Benin and could even offer suggestions to the world. He engages sympathetically and with humor with notions of boyhood, notions of Benin, and humane notions of interdependence.

STORIES THAT PROVOKE AESTHETIC RESPONSES: ASSESSMENT

When the time comes to assess the children's stories, we can assess them for how they incorporate the artifacts in ways that are historically informed. We can assess how they describe details that emerge from looking closely at the artifacts. We can assess whether their story lines reflect a relationship between the natural world and the human world, whether character and setting seem related in intimate ways that produce tension in the narrative. These elements, particular to this short story project, can make up our rubric. Ultimately, however, the children's stories are effective if they provoke aesthetic responses. Willie's story about the mud altar demonstrates a clear purpose. It incorporates the artifacts in informed ways, it demonstrates cultural knowledge, it relates setting to the characters' dilemmas in ways that produce tension. It is the underlying imaginative work, however, that shows Willie implicitly responding to the artifacts in aesthetic ways and creating a story that provokes his readers to similar aesthetic responses. Willie doesn't write his story from an outsider perspective. He imagines a perspective that was previously alien to him. And he does this so willingly and effectively that his story becomes a way to bring others into that perspective. Just as we can expect students to respond in aesthetic ways to art and to stories, I think we can expect our students to create work that has aesthetic potential.

Looked at this way, the work we did in this short story writing experience and cultural inquiry does not matter because the students learned to interpret artifacts, or they learned about Benin, or even because they learned to write some effective short stories, though these are good things to do in school. This work matters most because it is one way to learn what it feels like to engage sympathetically with notions of the other. It matters because shifting perspectives takes practice. It is easier to become rigid and closed than to become sympathetic and flexible in our perspectives. The children, however, show how they can imagine their emotional landscape as one that is potentially collective. Julia restructures her anxiety about faith as a vehicle for narrative tension in her story set in Benin. She is writing what she knows, but she is not writing only what she knows. Julia doesn't simply retell her story. She humanizes her story. She envisions that this story could exist in different ways in the world. Naomi Shihab Nye describes this as "our ability to grow in our perceptions, to know more than we used to know, to empathize with distant situations and sorrows and joys" (2002, introduction).

Another of the processes the children learn in this project is how to imagine the stories evoked by an object, by an image, by a scene that we have never seen before. This work in storytelling from a different cultural perspective matters because storytelling is one way ideas come to live in the world. And stories are a way we tutor our imaginations. In his declaration titled *Finished with the War: A Soldier's Declaration*, Sassoon rebuked the warmongers safe at home in 1917 for the "callous complacence" with which they regarded the "continuance of agonies which they do not share, and which they have not sufficient imagination to realize" (Hart-Davis 1994). Schooling needs to be a place where we develop sufficient imagination to envision the experience of all peoples as part of *our* experience. It needs to be a place where, in ways that seem minor and ways that seem marvelous, we consistently and continually seek humane ways to interact.

REFERENCES

Balick, D., and D. P. Wolf, eds. 1999. *Art Works! Interdisciplinary Learning Powered by the Arts*. Portsmouth, NH: Heinemann.

Bomer, R., and K. Bomer. 2001. *For a Better World: Reading and Writing for Social Action*. Portsmouth, NH: Heinemann.

Borges, J. L. 1988. *Labyrinths: Selected Short Stories and Other Writings*. New York: W. W. Norton.

Dewey, J. 1934. *The Need for a Philosophy of Education*. Chicago: University of Chicago Press.

Eisner, E. 1994. *Cognition and Curriculum Reconsidered*. New York: Teachers College Press.

Hart-Davis, R., ed. 1994. *The War Poems of Siegfried Sassoon*. London: Faber and Faber. (Accessed online at: www.oucs.ox.ac.uk/ltg/projects/jtap/tutorials/intro/sassoon/

Harwayne, S. 2001. *Writing Through Childhood: Rethinking Process and Product*. Portsmouth, NH: Heinemann.

hooks, b. 1994. *Teaching to Transgress: Education as the Practice of Freedom*. New York: Routledge.

Nye, N. S. 2002. *The Flag of Childhood*. New York: Aladdin Paperbacks.

Raouf, M. 1998. *Why Goats Smell Bad and Other Stories from Benin*. North Haven, CT: Linnet.

Sedgwick, E. 1990. *Epistemology of the Closet*. Berkeley: University of California Press.

Search Engines for Finding Cultural Artifacts

www.yahoo.com   Very helpful for finding museums, galleries, and exhibitions.

www.google.com   For finding articles and press releases.

www.amazon.com   Even if you are not going to purchase the books, this catalog helps you know what to look for at the library and to ask for on interlibrary loan.

Where to Find Images for Benin

Ezra, K. 1992. *The Royal Art of Benin: The Perls Collection*. New York: Metropolitan Museum of Art.

Metropolitan Museum of Art. 1987. *The Pacific Islands, Africa and the Americas*. New York: Metropolitan Museum of Art.

www.metmuseum.org   The website of the Metropolitan Museum of Art. Go to the arts of Africa, Oceania, and the America. This particular online collection is very limited though; the books are better in this study.

www.prm.ox.ac.uk/benin.html   The Pitt Rivers Museum of Oxford University. This site has historical and cultural information about Benin art, as well as images.

www.ou.edu/class/ahi1113/html/ch-15.htm   A section from an online art history class offered by the University of Oklahoma. Has some lucid images.

www.lam.mus.ca.us/africa/tour/benin/012.htm   Part of the Africa: One Continent: Many Worlds website. A plethora of images.

www.thebritishmuseum.ac.uk/compass   A website of the British Museum. Simply enter the collections and visit Benin to see many objects.

Chapter Four

Mythology and the Pedagogies of Desire

So I gave up fact and went to myth.
—William Stafford

Sometimes I am Daphne.
—Linda Pastan

I want to tell you, here, about a writing workshop in which we engage with the art forms of ancient sculpture and myth. It is a workshop where the role of the teacher as a writer and storyteller takes on grave and liberating implications in demonstrating mythic narrative possibilities. It is a workshop where the children think about how myths explain the way the world is, and how these explanations reflect ways of thinking about the world and our place in it. And it is a workshop where children come to realize that writing is a way to affect these notions. We can teach children to write joy into the world. We can teach them to describe sorrow, to illuminate loss, to envision change. When we teach children to write myth, we take up the very ways humankind has described its existence. When we begin with ancient sculptures, but hold on to the possibility that we may tell new myths from them, we create for children both a sense of historical perspective and a sense of narrative possibility. And so this chapter describes ways to look at sculptures, ways to tell myths, and particular ways to teach children that lead to purposeful, lucid, and liberating writing.

MYTH AND METAMORPHOSIS

Writing as an Act of Advocacy and as Part of Pedagogies of Desire

This is a workshop in which we examine the purpose of myth in order to consider the purpose of writing as a way of engaging with and restructuring the world. For it is not enough to instill a sense of craft in our students. What does it matter if they write well, unless in their writing there comes to be a sense of advocacy for themselves, for others, for the world they know and the world we wish we could have? When we teach myth, we teach children to express that advocacy in dreams—dreams of beauty, dreams of metamorphosis, dreams of desire. I want to enfold my students in dreams of love and passion and transformation. This is

93

why we write myths inspired by ancient sculpture. We dream dreams of the past, and these dreams are full of all of our present longings. In this workshop, we acknowledge that this world is simply not good enough and we put aside the everyday restraints that confine our ideas and our activities to the realistic. We dream mythic dreams, and we write in order to bring these dreams into the world. When I think of the racism, the homophobia, the sexism, the many forms of wanton and mundane cruelty that exist in the world, I know that schooling needs to be a place where we dream dreams of love.

And so in this workshop, we pay heed to ancient sculptures and to enduring dreams. We seek empathetic knowledge with these ancient sculptures, and through this process, with each other. When we write our myths, we come together to acknowledge the longings that are pressed underfoot in our everyday transactions. We actively seek stories that show we do not act alone. Stories of love. Stories of longing. We gather together to seek these stories, and in this gathering, we craft more than myth. We craft pedagogies of desire. Too often it seems we try to protect some notion of childhood as a state of innocence. Yet the children are witnessing, in many media, material saturated with sex, with sudden violence, with cruelty. What is frightening is that these performances are unaccompanied by passion, or pain, or the emotions that make us human, that attach meanings to these acts. We can reattach meaning in our storytelling. That is the ancient aim of myth, to attach meaning to events that are hard for us to understand. In his book *Romantic Understanding*, curriculum theorist Kieran Egan argues that middle school students in particular display marked tendencies toward romantic understanding, that leaning toward the transformative that marks the mythic. Students in early adolescence, Egan writes, "are bound by endless everyday constraints, and are relatively powerless to transcend them" (1990, 99). Adolescence *is* a state of desire and longing and dreams. It is the very nexus of myth.

When we ask students to write myths, we are asking them to explain the world around them. For that is the purpose of myth. And when I say explain the world, I do not mean explain why there are spiders. Ask them to explain homophobia. Ask them to explain racism. Ask them to explain the presence of joy or the nature of love. They live in this world. They participate in it. They need to see that their voices matter. When students engage with writing that matters, their writing begins to matter. And how much more swiftly their writing improves than when we simply focus on craft lessons. Their writing seems good because they are trying to say something important. There is a tacit response in the reader, a kind of emotional reaction that surges beyond the rational analysis of language skills. It is the same emotive response that art awakens in us, which is why we engage with myth here by engaging with sculpture. We could write myths by reading myths. But we want to write stories that have not yet been written. We want the unfettered dreams that imagine the human condition not only as it is known but as it could be known. When the ancient Greeks sculpted, they sculpted the human form and the human spirit. The models for the human form they used were limited by what they knew, but their imaginings of the human spirit were not. If we bring our dreams to these two thousand-year-old stones, we stir up a tempest of human longing. We participate in the urge to explain the way the world is, and we imagine that it can be a better place because we are here.

Orchestrating Environments of *Inter*dependence

It was conjointly with a group of middle school students that I first engaged with ancient sculptures in order to write myths, and I think this engagement has implications for incorporating curriculum development into our classroom practice as a means of acting together. I was taking an after-school group of middle school children to the sculpture galleries of the Metropolitan Museum for storytelling. We told stories in which the sculptures were characters, or that explained how the sculptures came to be, or that imagined the experience of the model or the artist. I told stories, the children told stories alone, we told stories collaboratively, and we rehearsed them so that there were small drama productions with only the sculptures as props. We expected our stories to be magical, and they were. We told ghost stories, folktales, and myths. As the children quickly became proficient at this activity, their oral storytelling skills, particularly in response to sculpture, came to far surpass their writing skills. Hoping to devise ways to shift these skills into writing, we decided to write our most ambitious stories, which were myths, and reflect on the experiences and structures that helped us write. In retrospect, I think that this is a model we can use more often. Our students have good ideas for curriculum sometimes, and if we teach them to plan for use of class time, resources, and what instruction they think they will need, they can join us as curriculum developers. We do not need to be in front and alone.

While this workshop has changed and continues to change, it is informed by the thinking of these initial students. As they worked to write their myths, this is what these middle school children decided they needed:

   to have access to the sculptures either in the galleries or through reproductions
   to have some assistance in looking at sculpture closely
   to hear some myths and to have some conversation about the elements of myths
   to have time to write
   to have some support in revision

And so the workshop follows an essential plan laid out by children. We devised instruction and support, we wrote, we worked alone at times but always in awareness of our collective purpose.

There is a way, in this incident of conjoint curriculum planning and writing, that we experienced what the educational philosopher John Dewey calls *interdependence.* Pointing out that we have romanticized *in*dependence as a quality, Dewey argues that

> there is always a danger that increased personal independence will decrease the social capacity of an individual. In making him more self-reliant, it may make him more self-sufficient; it may lead to aloofness and indifference. It often makes an individual so insensitive in his relations to others as to develop an illusion of being really able to stand and act alone—an unnamed form of insanity which is responsible for a large part of the remediable suffering of the world. (1916/1944, 44)

Ultimately, the work we did independently in writing our myths mattered because we were trying as a class to find dreams to dream and ways to write them. These middle school students, in seeking instruction and directing it, in acknowledging the needs and desires of their class, in engaging with the past through communion with art, orchestrated an experience of interdependence. In this process their writing took on an urgency beyond the personal.

This is where we see students engaged in writing that matters, when their concerns extend through writing practices to the social practices of conjoint living. Elai, an eighth grader, wrote a myth inspired by the sculpture the *Dying Gaul* (Figure 4–4, page 105), about two young warriors who love each other. When one dies in battle, the other stands over his fallen companion, protecting the body until he, too, is slain. Elai had a girlfriend and a cohort of friends made on the playing fields. In talking over his narrative with me, Elai said that he wanted to write a myth for his classmate David, because David seemed always alone. David was in the frightening process of coming out as a gay middle school student. David was teased sometimes, but mostly he simply existed in a silent abyss of uneasiness. Part of Elai's myth, which is reproduced in full in the Appendix (see page 150), reads:

> Alexander stood over Diomedes's body
> and looked at it with love and horror.
> Where was the wound?
> And then he saw the blood seeping from beneath the armor.
> A javelin must have pierced him
> under the arm where the leather parted.
> They taught the Gauls to look for the place.
>
> He stood over the body
> and decided that he would not leave this spot.
> And he raised his sword calmly
> to face the enemy rushing toward him.
> He brought ten of them with him into the dark
> And since that day

the Greeks save the Sacred Band, the legion of warrior-lovers
for their most desperate defenses
not because they are the most skilled warriors
but because they know the meaning of honor.

You can see that Elai has done some research about Greek armor, and that he remembered stories I had told about the Sacred Band, beloved of Alexander the Great. And you can see that he must have worked hard in revision to achieve such spare prose. You can imagine how he thought about word choice, about tense, about detail. His first draft did not look like this, and this craft makes his myth elegant and moving in a way that is surprising for an eighth grader. But the craft matters to me because it helps him achieve something else with his writing. Elai wrote love between men as a possibility into our classroom, and he linked this love with honor, with beauty, and with grace. He wrote for David. Writing workshop is more than minilessons on craft. We write to break down the illusion that we stand and act alone.

INTRODUCING PEDAGOGIES OF DESIRE

Desire informs the pedagogy of this workshop. It is with desire that I seek my students in the stories I tell. It is desire that informs our urge for knowledge and the need to tell our stories. Desire envelops all our dreams and longings for this world to be a different place. And it is potentially transformative desire, when it becomes collective. Elai's myth came into being in part in response to the myth I told, and our myths together helped engender a related myth by David. There is a way, when we tell stories, that we realize that concerns that we thought were personal are actually collective. And storytelling can also be a way that we imagine experiences we have not had personally so that they come to seem personal to us. As teachers, oral storytelling of myths is one way for us to orchestrate a collective experience. There is something about gathering a group of listeners around you—they not knowing what your story is going to be, and you willing yourself to the story—that puts you at a nexus of desire. You are the storyteller. You are the embodiment of the human urge to dream.

I want to tell you, now, the myth I tell my students, the myth that Elai had turned over in his head when he wrote his myth. For I, too, thought of David when I wrote my myth. I thought of all the ways that schooling becomes complicit with the policing of desire. I thought about homophobia and about what may be erotophobia in schooling, a sort of fear of acts of love and desire, and I thought I would tell a story that reattached meaning to these acts. I wanted to dream a dream of love, and it would not be a fairy tale, but a myth, where there are consequences for the choices we make, where our desires affect what happens in the world. It is a myth inspired by the sculpture *Statue of an Old Market Woman* (see Figure 4–1). It is a myth of a girl who loves a woman, and then a man, and it is of little consequence in the myth, the gender of the beloved, for myth allows us to ignore the rules of love that come to seem real in school cultures and society. I want to show, by storytelling, that there are other ways of knowing love than the ones we inherit. What is of consequence in *The Old Market Woman* is that we bc true to one another. Here is how I begin this myth. The entire myth is in the Appendix, on pages 161–68.

The Old Market Woman

On a mountaintop high above the Aegean
a girl dances in the moonlight.
Thalia of the flowing hair and graceful limbs.
Her hair is a cloud loose about her body.
Her eyes black in her pale face.
Her hands dart like birds about her.
She offers her body to Artemis of the silver bow,
goddess of the moon.
Her prayers are poems to a passion shared since childhood.

Oh virgin moon who bathes my limbs
Accept my gifts, forgive my sins
Artemisia my adored
beloved goddess, only lord

oh sister may I find you still
hunting love upon the hill
teach me to render in your tongue
the songs of ardor you have sung

The girl dances alone in the small clearing.
Her feet make intricate patterns in the dust.
Her slender limbs sway like young birches.
The moon blankets her in cool shadow
so that she is hidden from all else.
At last she bends backward
the white light caresses her,
she says farewell to her sister,
Artemis of the moon and the silver bow.

Oh sister how I still recall
the dark embrace behind the wall
pools of light behind your eyes
the voice of love where shadows lie

you pierce the heart in a virgin soul
fragment me yet keep me whole
oh faithful I shall ever be
to hill and moon and you and me

. . .

You can see even in the excerpt of "The Old Market Woman" that I read some Homer and some Ovid. You can see it in the attributes attached to the gods, in the repetitive phrasing and the use of verse. And you can see it in the treatment of desire. There is a thread running through the myth that is quietly but thoroughly antihomophobic. The verse seduces, and it is meant to. It exists in opposition to the way that much of young adult literature reiterates pathologies of the homosexual.

FIGURE 4–1   Statue of an Old Market Woman (detail)

Why are children's stories of homosexuality so often stories of great ugliness? When I read these stories, I am besieged by a sense of melancholia, the melancholia that feminist and gender scholar Judith Butler says accompanies the destruction of the homosexual (1990/1999). I think we have to pay attention to that melancholia, that sense of alienation, because it is undoubtedly felt, silently and oppressively, by students who are constrained by normative gender roles and sexual identities. And so one of the threads running through my story is the countenancing of desire, including homoerotic desire.

Narratives of desire unearth story lines that might otherwise be overwritten. In our eighth-grade classroom, David listens to my myth of Artemis and Elai's myth about young warrior-lovers. David's myth becomes a narrative about a boy who wanders the earth seeking to find the place where the gods have put love. Real love is sleeping, in the form of the sculpture *Statue of Eros Sleeping* (Figure 4–5). Only the boy knows that the thing that others think is love is a fraud, which is why the force of love is not strong enough for us to eliminate the borders that keep us separate. It is a mythic quest, in which the boy wants to set real love, which is held captive in a golden cage hanging from the sun, free in the world. Part of David's myth reads:

> When, when, when he wondered
> would he find the place where love was kept?
> If he could make the earth a place
> where it was safe to love
> the planets would still spin and the stars would still shine
> but the earth would stop rotating on its axis
> and jump out of its orbit for joy.

David is writing from the heart of a frightened middle school student who is coming out and who knows that schools are not safe places for gay students. He writes to expand existing notions of love. David is writing, in part, in response to the sculpture, and also in response to Elai's writing and my writing. In engaging the arts and writing myth, we are creating spaces of the imagination where David can find true love. We are writing story lines that make our existences possible. That is why I write for my students. Not to produce minilessons on craft, but because when we write, we write into existence many ways of knowing love. And in writing, we seek to bring other stories into the world.

Writing "The Old Market Woman," I am seeking my students. I want to wrap them in dreams of love. I dream with them about the siren call of beauty, the ache of unspoken desire, the urge toward transcendence and release. I want to tell them a story that is mythic in its proportions and human in its emotions. I return to the archaic language and the archaic purpose of Greek myth. Myths explain the known and suggest the unknowable. Myths remind us of the presence of the gods and our relations to them. Myths act as cautionary tales against hubris, the pride that leads humans to think themselves akin to the gods in knowledge.

When I read "The Old Market Woman" with my students, or when I perform it—for it is a performance—gathering the students close, with the image floating on an overhead screen, my voice low, enticing them to dream, we are at a point of convergence in the curriculum, a nexus where we are looking, we are dreaming, we are engaged with the ancient world and the modern. Myth does this. In myth all actions are initiated by human emotions. That is one reason myth is so enticing for early adolescents. It is the way, as Egan puts it, "the impossible has to conform with a kind of realistic plausibility" (1990, 87). It is the same tradition that informs comic book narratives and notions of the superhero. Write myths, for your students. Write what is real and what could be real. Write possibilities. Mythic narrative is a chance to unsettle those notions of adolescence and gender that can be so constraining in schooling. Dream desire in your myth. Dream liberation. Dream love in all its wondrous forms into your classroom.

WHY SCULPTURE WITH MYTH?

"The Old Market Woman" started with trying to know a sculpture. There is something about sculpture, something about the fullness of its form, the way it takes up space in the world, that evokes an answering physical response in our bodies. Somehow we know sculpture, especially large-scale sculpture, in a way that is different from knowing other works of art. It is easy to get around it, to notice it the way we notice our own bodies. And ancient sculpture is all about the body. Paleolithic sculpture exaggerates fecundity. Hindu sculpture can be pretty wildly erotic. Greek sculpture is often quite homoerotic. There is a kind of grace in the concept of the body as a thing of pleasure. In the later Greek sculptures, of the Hellenistic period, the body manifests the tribulations of the human spirit. I have a fondness for the sculpture of the old market woman because she seems so enduring. With her back bent, her tired arm clutching the basket full of chickens, she plods on. To me she shows as much physical courage as the sculptures of young warriors and athletes so common in the Greek Classical period. And she hints at something else also: that fear hidden in all of us, not only of old age but of old age combined with poverty. I wonder, as I look at her, about the artist who was willing to portray the slow decaying of the body and the human fortitude that withstands that ancient process. And perhaps my story comes, in part, from an urge to hold off that age forever.

Like Greek sculpture, Greek myth is grounded in human experience. Myth explains the ordinary and dreams the extraordinary. And it is important that we make space in the curriculum for these dreams. When we allow for dreams of metamorphosis, we imagine in schooling what seems impossible in the world. And so the writing of myth is part of a larger educational purpose, one that is involved in reaching beyond present experiences. "Education," writes Egan in *Imagination in Teaching and Learning*, "is a process that awakens individuals to a kind of thought that enables them to imagine conditions other than those that exist or that have existed" (1992, 46). We awaken that kind of thinking when we engage students with myth. When we engage them through sympathetic response to a sculpture, we also do something else: we foster sympathetic understanding as a way of knowing. And it is this sympathetic understanding that informs the social processes of living in humane communities.

Dewey names the quality of sympathy as the cornerstone of social living, and he names schools as places where we may activate sympathy, in the classroom (1916/1944). That is what I see us doing when we engage students with ancient sculpture and with myth. We are cultivating a humanistic imagination. We are concerned with what makes us human. When we imagine myth through ancient sculpture, we look backward, but it is to a past intimately linked to the present and to our present concerns. We look to know and we write to know, and it is humanistic knowledge that we seek. "Knowledge is humanistic in quality," writes Dewey, "not because it is *about* human products in the past, but because of what it *does* in liberating human intelligence and human sympathy" (1916/1944, 230). Thinking of schooling, curriculum, and literacy as liberating processes makes our work matter. It makes the work of teaching writing matter in the work of the world.

WHY GREEK SCULPTURE?

I like to work with Greek sculpture for this workshop because of its close narrative relationship with myth and because humanism arose with the Greeks. In all the arts the Greeks focused on the human experience, and in sculpture especially they focused on the human body as a vehicle for expressing the human experience. The Greeks were the first to create art solely to describe and to elevate the human condition. In the godlike perfection of young athletes and warriors, they paid tribute to courage, strength, and fortitude, and they linked these qualities with notions of grace and beauty. While sculpting a classical form of humanism, the Greeks also sculpted enduring Western notions of masculinity. There is a book called *The Image of Man*, in which the author, Mosse, looks at why Greek sculpture continues to exert itself as an ideal of beauty. He notes that the Greeks sculpted "young athletes who through the structure of their bodies and their comportment exemplified power and virility, and also harmony, proportion, and self-control . . . the ideal body projected both strength and restraint" (1996, 29).

My students often are drawn to Classical sculptures; they are enticed and uplifted by the blending of beauty and heroism. But the Greeks did more than extol ideals of beauty. The Greeks ultimately forsook the Classical perfection that made every male an athlete or a warrior and every woman a sublime vessel. Hellenistic sculpture, the later sculpture, abandons the restraints of Classical form and notions of the heroic. In the Hellenistic period, artists turned to the imperfections, the fears, the uncertainties that make us human and that make our strengths significant and our joys meaningful. They sculpted moments of great cruelty, and great tenderness, they looked at how we try to hold off death, at how we hurt each other, at how we love. I prefer Hellenistic sculpture for its variety of form and for the way it explores the human experience with more sympathy than does sculpture of the Classical period.

Greek sculpture of any period is particularly accessible in stimulating children to write. One reason is that it is human, in its subject matter, in its realism, often even in its size. Another reason is that Greek sculpture is laden with narrative possibility. Greek sculptures were made to acclaim, to inspire, and to instruct. They are suggestive. Just glance through a book of Greek sculptures or go to the websites of the museum collections noted at the end of this chapter. You will see women dancing, men poised for the discus throw or the javelin thrust, adolescent boys preening, warriors marking a grave, infants sleeping, couples embracing a child, the old market woman making her slow way uphill. The Greeks made sculpture in order to tell part of a mythic story, or to remind us of the part played

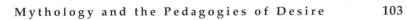

FIGURE 4–2   Artemis the Huntress/Diana of Versailles

FIGURE 4–3   Statue of an Old Market Woman

FIGURE 4–4   Dying Gaul

in a human story by the figure represented by the sculpture. So the narratives are almost waiting for us. These dancing women and eager warriors and sleepy children are poised, waiting to play their part in our stories, waiting to suggest forgotten story lines, to remind us they are here, still, an ancient presence in our world. Figures 4–2 through 4–7 show some of the sculptures we look at when preparing to write myths. These images are available through links on the companion website (*www.heinemenn.com/ehrenworth*). Many others are available through the websites listed at the end of the chapter.

STARTING WITH A MYTHIC STORY

When I want to enter the world of dreams that is Greek myth, I turn to three books that sit on the shelf above my desk. They are Edith Hamilton's *Mythology* (1950); Allen Mandelbaum's *Metamorphoses of Ovid* (1993); and Richmond Lattimore's *Iliad and Odyssey of Homer* (1977). In these books are all the tales of courage and sacrifice, greed and envy, desire and despair that Homer and the Greeks first invented thousands of years ago. But I riffle these pages not so much for the narratives as for the language. It is a language full of imagery and metaphor. Swift-footed Achilles. Hektor of the shining helm. Patroklos the blameless. Listen to Homer telling us how, in front of the walls of Troy, the Greeks fought to protect the body of the fallen Patroklos, staunch companion of the haughty Achilles:

> So they fought on in the likeness of fire, nor would you have thought
> the sun was still secure in his place in the sky, nor the moon, since
> the mist was closed over all that part of the fight where the bravest
> stood about Patroklos, the fallen son . . .
> So they about the body gripping their headed spears kept
> inexorably close together, and slaughtered on both sides . . .
> So they fought on, and the iron tumult
> went up into the brazen sky through the barren bright air
> (Book 17, lines 366–69, 412–13, 424–25)

It is Troy, it is Verdun, it is Dunkirk and all the battles men have raged against each other where they slaughtered on both sides until the very planets seemed insecure in their places. And it is poetry, which is the language of myth. Listen now to the Roman poet Ovid retelling the Classical myth of Daphne. Daphne, who was pursued by relentless Apollo and, fleeing, called aloud to be saved and was transformed into the laurel tree, which still trembles in fear in the presence of men:

> Love has given wings to the pursuer;
> he's faster—and his pace will not relent.
> He's at her shoulders now; she feels his breath
> upon the hair that streams down to her neck.
> Exhausted, wayworn, pale, and terrified,
> she sees Peneus' stream nearby; she cries:
> "Help me dear father; if the river-gods
> have any power, then transform, dissolve
> my gracious shape, the form that pleased too well!"
> As soon as she is finished with her prayer,
> a heavy numbness grips her limbs; thin bark
> begins to gird her tender frame, her hair
> is changed to leaves, her arms to boughs; her feet—
> so keen to race before—are now held fast
> by sluggish roots; the girl's head vanishes,
> becoming a treetop.
> (Book 1:24, lines 543–58)

It is every woman who has denied a man and found herself powerless, who has fought, and fled, and yet found herself trapped, who in that terrible moment has

FIGURE 4–5   Statue of Eros Sleeping

dreamed of transformation and of escape, wishing only to be out of this body that has betrayed her with its weakness, and out, entirely, of the world of men. "Sometimes I am Daphne," writes the poet Linda Pastan (1982, 52). Sometimes we too may find we are Daphne, caught up in someone else's story line, having lost control of our own. Daphne's metamorphosis is a metaphor for how we regenerate ourselves. We dream ourselves anew. It is this language, rich with metaphoric possibility, that we can saturate our myths with. We dream caterpillar dreams, bringing into our classrooms the latent, suggestive potential of metamorphosis.

I give you some Homer and some Ovid since this may be all the Homer and Ovid you want to start with. You don't need to redo all the work I did in becoming familiar with myth. I hope you will take this work forward, imagine new possibilities. Appropriate "The Old Market Woman." Change it, revise it, adapt it to work for your classroom. You may have other concerns you want to metamorphose. If you would like to write your own myth as a model, or when you write

FIGURE 4–6   Statuette of a Veiled and Masked Dancer

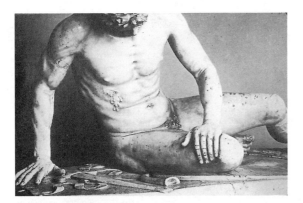

FIGURE 4–7   Dying Gaul (detail)

your myth alongside your students in the writing workshop, it is probably helpful to be familiar with Edith Hamilton's *Mythology* as a way to know the common attributes and characters of the Greek gods. And glance through Homer or Ovid if you would like to get more of a feeling for their metaphoric and figurative language. But look most intensely for what Hamilton, and Homer, and Ovid don't say. It is in the places where the narratives elide, where there is slippage and incoherency, that our narratives reside.

This is often how I help children find ideas for their stories. Look at the sculptures. Look to what the myths don't explain. We don't have all the stories. They were not translated, or they were lost, or they never existed. When I read about Artemis, for example, I am intrigued by how Homer and Ovid hint at a kind of latent desire between the twins Artemis and Apollo. I imagine how this desire could complicate their relationship with each other and interfere with humans. I look at the sculptures, and I imagine what these sculptures are trying to tell us. I may start this mythology workshop with "The Old Market Woman." But I may start by putting on an overhead the image of *Artemis the Huntress* from the Louvre. I put the lights down low, and gather the children close. And I say something like:

In the time of the long-dead Homer, the bards would visit the villages and towns of Greece to tell the stories of the gods and the tales of the heroes. We remember their stories from the versions that were written later, and from the sculptures and temples, paintings and vases that survive. They told of Zeus the omnipotent, and of Achilles the champion, and of the long fought battle for Troy. But the tales they told were a male history, told by poets who spoke for generations of men. I like to imagine, though, that there were female bards who told the forgotten histories of the goddesses and the women of Greece. To these women, Zeus was a faithless consort, and Achilles a sulky child. They told the female tales, and these tales were dark at times, cautionary tales for this world of men.

Such a story is this, told by a female bard. This bard relates myths known and unknown, and creates new ones of her own, and she tells these tales as a woman would, seeking to draw in the women who sit at the outskirts of the circle when the bard visits. Some of these women add to the story, telling poems forgotten or tales of sculptures long destroyed. Some of the men tell answering tales, seeking to reclaim their knowledge of the world. This is a story of love and desire, death and betrayal, vengeance and loss. It is the story of the most female of the Olympian immortals, who asked Zeus to let her remain ever a maiden and not be forced into marriage, Artemis the huntress, goddess of the moon. She was born a twin to Apollo. They were the children of Zeus and of Leto. They were

*born on Mount Olympos, and both were given silver bows at birth. And Artemis became
the goddess of the moon and Apollo the god of the sun, and never shall they meet in the
sky, though Apollo chases his sister endlessly. For the rules of love we have made for
humans do not apply to the gods.*

Looking up, sometimes, at the image of *Artemis the Huntress*, I read, slowly, a
myth, this one short, as they sometimes can be:

Artemis the Huntress

She was born of thundering Zeus and Leto of the lovely hair
a day before her brother Apollo,
so she could assist her mother with his birth.
Twin children with silver bows.
Artemis of the falling arrows,
Apollo who strikes from afar.
They took a vow to be true to each other
and so they were
entwined on the mountain
Artemis of the evening moon
Apollo of the rising sun
The archers
incandescent in ardor on dark-clouded Olympos.
But Artemis guarded her virgin maidenhead
even from her shining brother
and Apollo sought the pale embrace of earthly maidens
ever seeking knowledge of his moon-bright silver sister.
Looking darkly at her twin, Artemis of the falling arrows
turned from men, and stepped alone into the forest.
She became the huntress, a guardian of wild beasts
and the girls who prayed to her.
Adorned by the crescent moon in her hair
and the quiver on her back
she gathered a band of nymphs and maidens
and led them through secluded streams and sacred groves.
Still she hunts alone, with her swift-footed dogs
Artemis of the silver bow and the white arms,
and the heart divided within her
since its split from shining-eyed Apollo.

If we want the children to believe in dreams, we have to show ourselves dreaming. I tell "The Old Market Woman" another day, and I tell other stories of Artemis
and Apollo, Artemis and Actaeon, Artemis as Diana. I dream Artemis into our
classroom. I return to her again and again, so that our classroom is a web of love

and desire and passionate choices. And always, I imagine the consequences of these choices. I reattach meaning that has been dissolved in the superficial story lines of popular culture. And I show the students how I start with the sculpture *Artemis the Huntress*. We look at the image, and I note how solitary Artemis looks, how she seems so intimate with the stag but so isolated from humans. I note the bow and arrows and quiver, and I include these in my myth. I see the crescent moon in her hair and include that also. I see how young she is, and how graceful and strong. And it is surprising that such a beautiful creature would be so alone. And so my myth is going to be about how Artemis came to be alone, and she will wear the crescent moon and hunt with the animals in the woods. I am showing the students how we look, we imagine, we write. I dream with them.

LEARNING CENTERS FOR HISTORICAL RESEARCH

I also remind the students that I know something about Greek myth. It may be helpful, I suggest, if before we begin to write our own myths we know something collectively about Greek mythology, including some of the gods and goddesses and tales. I often pursue historic inquiry in upper elementary and middle school through four or five learning centers set up around the room. The students rotate through the centers in small groups. At each center we gather together resources about a certain aspect of our inquiry, and the students engage in an activity. For instance, one center may have several picture books, and even a paper doll book, on Greek clothing, and the students have to design their own clothing and show how it demonstrates their position in Greek society—and put their creations up on the wall as resources for other students. Another may have many resources on the gods and goddesses, and the students collectively have to make a family tree for our classroom wall, an annotated diagram that includes illustrations and the attributes of the gods and goddesses. In another they may interpret a Greek myth through performance.

In making learning centers, it is crucial to gather resources that the students may use independently, which means the reading level must be accessible. I have listed some useful ones in the "References" section of this chapter. Don't be afraid that they seem so easy. Meaningful research does not mean taking notes from a difficult text. Research means looking at how people share information and ideas and then making something ourselves with this material. It is in the activity that the students construct meaning. I try to design learning center activities in which the students are making things we will use collectively and independently in our next activity, which in this case will be writing our myths. We all need a reference source for the gods. Depending on what their myths are about, they may need to be informed about clothing, or Greek society, and they may seek each other out when they know who is an expert on the clothing or on the daily life of foot soldiers, and who on society matrons. The students participate in the activities, and they also become familiar with the references that they may return to when they are writing their myths. We interrupt our progress periodically to share our activities with the class as a whole. For instance, we put up and explain our diagrams and drawings. We perform our interpretations of particular myths and explain to the class why we chose the myths we did and what we think these myths are trying to say.

Learning centers that the children participate in and add to are an effective way to orchestrate experiential learning and to build collective knowledge. Anytime we are writing texts or making projects that are meant to be historically informed, I usually set up learning centers for one or two weeks. My students have written myths without this step. But it makes for a lot of work later in revision when we want the narratives to feel authentic. Or you simply end up telling the students things, which is certainly easy but probably not so helpful in terms of them becoming autonomous in their learning. We want them to know what the work is that writers do to give their writing integrity. And part of that work is research.

LOOKING FOR *NARRATIVE POSSIBILITIES* AND *DETAIL*

We start the workshop by looking at an image of a sculpture and storytelling a myth that revolves around this sculpture. Then the children may participate in learning centers, which may overlap with what we do now, which is to look at many sculptures. I give the children access to as many images as possible. If you are in a school with Internet access, you may download them from museum websites. Just click your mouse on the image, save the picture to a drive, and you have your own archive from which you can print images. I also get books from the library, or I bring my own books, and we make copies. Two useful books are Boardman's *Greek Sculpture* (1985), and Smith's *Hellenistic Sculpture* (1991), both of which are inexpensive and easy to find in bookstores. There is also a beautiful book called *Greek Sculpture: An Exploration*, by Andrew Stewart (1990). It has gorgeous photographs, including close details, of almost all the large-scale Greek sculpture in the world. Unfortunately, it is horrendously expensive. But you can have your library get it on loan and just make a series of copies from it. Greek sculptures, while they were often originally painted, are now monochrome, so that black-and-white reproductions serve our purpose admirably. I keep an original set of copies in plastic slipcovers and then just make class copies from these.

When we begin looking at the sculptures, we are looking in two ways. I tell the children that first, we are looking for the *narrative possibilities* of the sculpture. For instance, David saw that Eros (the god of love, also known as Cupid) was sleeping. He imagined what happened in the world of humans when Eros slept and constructed a narrative where Eros is asleep in a golden cage while a malicious impersonator makes mischief with humans. That is imagining narrative possibility. Elai looked at the *Dying Gaul* and imagined a narrative about how young warriors came to be wounded in battle. Sometimes the children may imagine more abstract or metaphoric possibilities. In the collection of the Metropolitan Museum, there is a small sculpture of a veiled woman dancing, called *Statuette of a Veiled and Masked Dancer*. Sixth grader Stephanie wondered why this woman was dancing and what happened when she danced. She imagined that this woman was given a gift by the gods so that when she danced, rivers of joy spread from her feet and whole villages started celebrations from which they emerged, breathless and wondering, only when the woman paused.

Looking for narrative possibilities means looking for stories. The best way to help the children with this is simply to listen. If it is not easy for them to write, write down as much as you can of what they say, and simply hand it over to them as jottings they can build their story from. Partnerships are good for this activity also. Some children like to freewrite immediately. Mostly, though, we are rehearsing our stories orally. Some students focus immediately on a single sculpture, others like to try storytelling with a few, and some may incorporate more than one sculpture in their stories. I let them follow their natural inclination, and I simply listen to them. When we listen, we create a sense of audience for children. This is tremendously important. I think it may be the most important thing we do in writing workshop.

The second way we are looking is *looking for detail*. This is where you can help the children notice details like clothing, adornment, what the figure is carrying, any weapons or wounds, the posture, facial expression, how the hair is done, how the body holds itself. Get the children to jot down all the details they notice. Also, ask them about the overall mood of the sculpture. Does it seem proud? Secretive? Arrogant? Humble? Mischievous? Anxious? Ask the children to write down all the details that make them think the sculpture has this overall effect.

When we notice detail, we are noticing the vocabulary of sculptural form. If the children describe what they see in detail, inevitably the residue of this form makes its presence felt in their written narrative, so that some of the evocative powers of the original artist become theirs. In describing Eros in his myth, for instance, David *looks* and writes that:

> Eros was asleep on a stone in a golden cage
> His body folded onto the rock as if it were the softest cushion.
> His eyes were closed, his mouth open,
> his legs and arms seemed heavy with the
> weight of their soft chubbiness.
> Not even the feathers of the wings that grew out of his back
> or the curls of his short hair
> moved as he slept.
> He knew it was Eros because his heart
> was filled with love at the sight of the child.

David, you can see, tells both what the sculpture looks like and the effect the sculpture has on the viewer. For David, looking for detail becomes looking for narrative possibility. It matters in David's narrative that the figure of Eros causes the heart to fill with love, for while Eros is absent, love is absent from the world.

I may help the children make something of their looking by having them do an observation chart in their notebooks. In this chart they jot down what they see, what they think, and what they wonder as they look at the sculpture. Usually the children complete the first column in detail first, and then they can work on the other two, building on their noticings in the first column. On the following page is Jenny's observation chart for *Statue of an Old Market Woman.*

The details that are in italics were not in Jenny's chart the first time. When she read her notes to me, I asked her: Where are there wrinkles? Where are there lines of pain? Where is she broken? What is in the basket? Can you look again and pretend you are describing the sculpture in detail to someone who cannot see it but wants to draw it? She added the italicized details. Jenny will be able to use these details in her writing, and she'll have a better feel for the effect of the sculpture because she looked more closely. You can see how Jenny has some stuff to start with now, especially when looking for detail leads her to wonder if the woman is stronger than she really looks, or if her body does not reflect the strength or beauty of her spirit. That is where, if I have a conference with her, I may ask Jenny if she can imagine a myth that would show those ideas. We could use more stories that examine beauty of spirit rather than female form. But Jenny has lots of narrative possibilities in this chart, and she may choose something else. She is wondering how the sculpture came to be smashed, if someone hated this woman. There is a story there. She is wondering if the woman will choose not to kill the chickens. There could be a story there. She is thinking that the chickens could be a religious offering. Another story.

Charting is simply a way for the children to record their observations in a manner that helps suggest narrative possibilities. It is also useful because you can also see from the What I Think column if the students need to know more. For instance, Jenny could probably use some information about how and when the Greeks made offerings. If part of her myth is going to be set in a temple or a market, she may want illustrations of these places. The students can also simply jot down noticings in their notebooks. They can do noticings on one page, and wonderings on the opposite, and they may sketch some of the details. And sometimes the students want to simply start freewriting or doing oral storytelling and come back for details later. I do ask my students to look at details before drafting, though, because I want them to develop a rigorous eye. Also, I don't really want them to draft until we have talked about narrative purpose and structure. In this workshop, I want them to know what it feels like to write with knowledge and with intent.

What I See	What I Think	What I Wonder
She is small, under life-size Her skin is wrinkled *at the neck and the corners of her eyes and around her mouth* There are lines of pain *above her mouth*	She seems like she was petite She is very old She is in pain, her body hurts	Was she pretty once?
Her collarbone sticks out hard She seems really thin She has kind of ropy muscles, stringy, *in her arms* Her back is bent	She seems hungry She seems poor She is strong even though she is so thin	Is she all alone? Does she have to carry stuff a lot? Will she be able to do it? Is she strong? Is she more strong than she looks, or is her spirit strong enough for anything? Is she beautiful inside?
She wears some kind of dress, belted but it is coming loose so you can see her chest all loose and floppy And she wears some kind of robe maybe but it is loose too	She must only have these clothes It is so hard to walk that she can't bother with the clothes	
She is broken. *The nose is broken off, and one arm, and her face is damaged.* She holds a basket, *with chickens or something with feathers.*	She has been damaged, maybe someone tried to smash her She is going or coming from market. Or maybe a temple? The chickens look scrawny like her.	Does someone hate her? What does she do? Will she make it to market, and what will happen there? Will she really kill the chickens? Are the chickens an offering?

TEACHING *NARRATIVE PURPOSE* AND *NARRATIVE STRUCTURE*

When the students are intimate with their sculptures and they have imagined some narrative possibilities, they are ready to move from freewriting and oral storytelling to drafting myths. I remind them of the common purposes of Greek myths, including to

> explain how something exists in the world—either how it came to be or what it does (like the myth of Daphne or of Apollo driving the sun)
> affirm relations among humans, the gods, and the natural world (like the myth of Persephone)
> teach us something about human behavior by exalting the heroic and punishing the wicked and those guilty of hubris (like the myth of Hercules, or Midas, or Arachne)

I might chart these purposes with the students. I am not looking to formalize these categories; what I want is for the students to understand that myths are purposeful. So before we draft, we need to think about *narrative purpose*. I don't make this a formal minilesson, because the children might think that all myths fall into these categories, and they don't. Any single myth may do any of these things, and more, or something else. Teaching in this area falls, for me, under literary conversation in the classroom. We chart some of the common purposes. I read aloud or storytell Greek myths. We interpret their purposes, and I encourage the children to expand their notion of purpose from our original list. I ask them to listen not for what the myth tells them, but for what it doesn't, or even for what it may be misrepresenting. Is Apollo really a victim of Cupid's mischievous arrow, so that he is helpless to resist Daphne? What if the myth is told this way in order to make acceptable masculine aggression, to justify the existence of rape and mayhem? What if a woman told the story—would it be different? I am nudging the children to pose questions about why the myths are told in certain ways.

The next step is to see that if we pose these questions when we listen, then we should pose the same questions when we write. It is often a new idea for children that if we want our myths to lead to certain understandings, we need to write these understandings into our narratives. If we want our myths to unsettle, then we must write unsettling narratives. If we want our myths to soothe certain fears, then we must write narratives of comfort. So we need to think about purpose before we start drafting. This I do make a very direct minilesson. I explain that we need to ask: What do I want my story to do? In "The Old Market Woman," I want to unsettle heterosexist notions of desire and sexuality. David wants to show that the ideas of love that exist in the world are incomplete. Elai wants to affirm homosexuality as a site of honor. We are writing to each other, Elai, and Dave, and I. Our purpose is the delicate weaving of antihomophobia into classroom artifacts.

I have found that it is usually good for students to reflect alone about the question, What do I want my story to do? It is possible that their purpose may emerge as something so deeply felt that they cannot bear to share it, in such a bare form, with their peers. Elai, for instance, was not willing to talk in partnership about the purpose that was in his heart, which was to show homosexuality as honorable. So when he conferred with me, I asked him what kind of myth would help him tell this story, and he decided it would be a myth that would teach us something about human behavior. That, he could talk about with his peers. That his narrative would exalt heroism as a form of love between men would emerge in the telling.

As the children choose various purposes for their myths, we can help them articulate their purpose by teaching them about *narrative structure*. I do a minilesson explaining that narrative structure is directly related to narrative purpose. If they choose to explain how something came to be, the way the myth of Daphne explains the existence of the laurel tree, for instance, then their narrative structure should probably be "it doesn't exist, something happens to make it exist, it exists." Narrative structure is the way we articulate purpose. Daphne is a girl. She flees Apollo's lust and begs to be saved. She is turned into the laurel tree. I find this a comfortless tale, but its narrative structure is clear and purposeful.

Clarifying narrative structure is extraordinarily helpful in making the children's writing purposeful and helping them get started. After the minilesson, this teaching has to continue in conferring with all students about their purposes. If their purpose is to teach proper behavior, then the structure is this: The character behaves in a certain way. The character is rewarded or punished. A lesson is learned. If they have a metaphoric purpose, such as Stephanie's notion that the dancing woman is the embodiment of joy, then they begin with a narrative structure that demonstrates the metaphor. Stephanie needs to show what happens when the woman dances. Her narrative structure will be simple: The woman is not dancing. There is no joy in the world. She dances. Something joyful happens. David's structure, which also demonstrates a metaphor, is this: There is no real love in the world. Someone finds that Eros is captive and asleep. He realizes why there is no real love.

Planning structure does not mean we do not make discoveries and choices as we write. David didn't know as he was writing his myth whether Eros would be set free or would remain a captive. But he knew his myth would suggest that he does not know the world as a home for true love. My structure for "The Old Market Woman" is the "something comes to exist" structure. Thalia is a girl, something happens (she scorns Apollo, and loves him, she loves Artemis, and forsakes her), and she is turned to stone as an old woman, thus bringing the sculpture into existence. It was as I was telling the story that I wove narratives of desire into this structure. Narrative structure does not limit the power of our myths. Narrative structure simply helps us articulate our myths in a purposeful way.

WRITING MYTH

Drafting

You will notice that I am not saving discussions of purpose and structure for revision. It is too hard to revise a draft that is written without intent. Here is where we are, *as we begin writing*. We have chosen our sculpture, we have looked at it carefully, and we continue to look at it. We have looked at it for details and to imagine some narrative possibilities. We may have been doing some writing in our notebooks or some storytelling with partners. We may have been involved in learning centers. We have been listening to myths. We have thought about what kind of myth we would like to tell. We have outlined our narrative structure.

Now we write. This is where having a simple structure in mind really helps. Even if we abandon it later, or it becomes secondary to a larger purpose, it helps us get started. Write with your students. Choose your sculpture. Look closely at the details. Art is an experience of immanence. Commune with this ancient artifact. Dream mythic dreams. Even if the myth you write is not intended for classroom use, you will not be the same teacher of writing after you write it. Try the writing lessons you are teaching. Articulate the purpose and structure of your myth. Or jettison this book and just read Ovid and look at sculpture. What matters is that we, too, engage with myth. This means that we have integrity as teachers of writing. It also means that we, too, grow and learn and dream.

Conferring

As the students draft, confer with them. Most of my meaningful teaching of writing happens in conferring. It is personal. It is teaching that is addressed to this particular writer at this particular time. I think of conferences generally in two ways. Initially my aim in conferences is to maintain enthusiasm for writing. Perhaps the most useful thing I do in conferences is name for the writer some of what I see the writer doing. Eighth grader David had an initial freewrite in his notebook, written as he looked at the sculpture *Statue of Eros Sleeping*:

> It is a baby sleeping only it's not a baby, it's the god of love, Cupid.
> He is sleeping on a rock. He looks drugged. I wonder if he is okay.
> Maybe someone needs to rescue him, maybe he has been kidnaped [sic].
> I wonder what happens if he is the god of love and he is sleeping—is love asleep? Maybe we should wake him up.

When we conferred, David didn't know what he could do with this entry, and he was unsure if he could write about a baby. I said, "I can see some qualities of a quest narrative here—do you know about the quest in literature? There is rather an epic flavor to this, even though it is just a freewrite." Telling the students what they *are* doing can be very powerful for them.

Fifth grader Stephanie's freewrite about the *Veiled Dancer* looked like this:

> she is swirling and turning
> she holds vails over her face
> she spins like a top
> I would love to dance like that
> all swirly and wild

Stephanie already had a contemporary free verse poem, and I told her that. She preened a little. She didn't know what she could do though; she couldn't see how a myth could come from what she saw and felt. I said, "When I read your verse, it reminds me of the myths that are metaphoric, like Pandora's box letting lies into the world. It sounds, from your freewrite, Stephanie, as if when you see this woman dancing, something happens."

Stephanie said, "Mmm-hmm, you want to dance too. She makes me happy. I want to dance with her."

I said, "Okay, so let me restate what you just said in a way that would describe a narrative structure. When Pandora opened this box, lies came into the world. What comes into the world when this woman dances?"

"Happiness, no, joy," said Stephanie.

"Okay, so can you write a myth that shows joy coming into the world when this woman dances?" That is conferring that is about naming for the kids when they are doing, or are on the edge of doing, something powerful in their writing.

So when I say confer to stimulate enthusiasm, I envision the children becoming enthusiastic about their writing because they see their writing becoming powerful. Another purpose of conferences is to help our students get out of places where they are stuck or to push them to new levels. I might advise them to do an observation chart. I might jot down their ideas as they speak. I might show them some Ovid, or some Homer, or some student writing. Often I simply listen intensely to provide an audience. Sometimes I can also see that a lesson on craft may lift their writing to a new level.

Craft Lessons

There are just a few craft lessons that I associate with writing myth. I usually save these lessons until the students have had plenty of time to write with the sculptures. So you may choose to introduce some of these craft lessons when you talk about revision. They have to do with the language of myth. When we read Homer and Ovid, we are reading verse. So I remind the children of this during our first craft lesson. Verse makes the myth more beautiful on the page and to the ear. When we write in verse, it helps us keep our language spare and our imagery significant. I tell the children that one reason I think the versions of the myths that have been adapted for children are so much less powerful than the originals is that they have been translated into prose. I show them some excerpts from Homer and Ovid—perhaps the ones mentioned earlier about the death of Patroklos and the transformation of Daphne. The language of Homer is hard, so I also show them some excerpts that give a sense of its passion and its sometimes harsh brightness. I may show the children the following excerpt, when Achilles is grieving for Patroklos, who has been slaughtered by Hektor. Achilles cries out over the body of Patroklos:

> I will not bury you till I bring to this place the armour
> and the head of Hektor, since he was your great-hearted murderer.
> Before your burning pyre I shall behead twelve glorious
> children of the Trojans, for my anger over your slaying.
> Until then, you shall lie where you are in front of my curved ships
> and beside you women of Troy and deep-girdled Dardanian women
> shall sorrow for you night and day and shed tears for you, those whom
> you and I worked hard to capture by force and the long spear
> in days when we were storming the rich cities of mortals.
> (Book 18, lines 334–42)

Children are naturally mimetic. Elai wrote in prose but then transformed it to verse in revision. This process actually works well. They can get the structure of their narrative in place in prose and then reinvent it in verse. The language of Elai's myth in verse is not dissimilar to Homer's. It has the same rather hard tone, which is such a brilliant match for his purpose—to make homosexuality an acceptable form of masculinity. This is the moment in Elai's myth when one of his heroes, his young warrior-lovers, is killed. Elai writes:

> Back to back the two boys fought
> Each protecting the other
> Iron swords clashing
> Calling only to each other
> Until Apollo, the lord who strikes from afar
> jealous of this devotion
> guided the iron-tipped spear of a Gaul
> to the tender place above Diomedes's heart
> and Apollo's javelin entered also
> and Diomedes fell in the dust.

I can see that Elai's writing is informed by a second craft lesson I presented, which looked at the way Homer and Ovid attach attributes to persons and gods. That is a characteristic of myth and of epic tales that were told orally. The attributes are descriptive, and they are repeated whenever the character appears. When Apollo appears in *The Iliad*, he may be named as Apollo or as Phoibos or as the son of Zeus or the sun-god. But he will also be named as the lord or god who strikes from afar. So the attribute helps the listener recognize Apollo, and it also describes him. Apollo hunts with arrows, and in combat, he throws a javelin. He is also relentless in seeking revenge. Apollo strikes from afar.

I simply read aloud to the children some of the ways the gods and heroes are named. Hera of the lovely arms. Artemis of the falling arrows. Gray-eyed Athene. Apollo, the lord who strikes from afar. The children may choose to incorporate these terms in their myths. Or they may invent their own attributes for the characters of their myths. There will be an archaic flavor to their language. The residue of Ovid and Homer makes itself felt in the same way the residue of the sculptor's art makes itself felt in our descriptions of the sculptures. You can see how Elai appropriates Homer's way of describing Apollo and how this appropriation adds an unexpected archaic flavor to Elai's language. Elai has only glimpsed Homer when I read aloud the one or two passages that I thought might reach the children despite the unfamiliar vocabulary and story. But a glimpse of Homer will lift our writing.

Homer also depends on repetition. Phrases that describe events, persons, or places are repeated throughout the epic poem. Somehow this repetition gives a kind of lilting music to the poetry. Sixth grader Stephanie picks up this use of repetition in her myth, which I have presented in full in the Appendix, on page 149, when she repeats the phrases about the villagers picking olives and about their backs hurting. Also, this repetition means that the myths are not introducing new images very often. A set of images often runs throughout a myth, creating patterns and containing the myth for the listener. I may suggest to the students that they discipline their myths this way. It gives the myth a kind of archaic formalism.

Revision

Aside from these craft lessons, which I may introduce as students are revising, I have found that revision of myth usually means revisiting our writing to make it more spare. Look to see if the children have let themselves wander far from the sculpture or far from their narrative structure. I ask the children to think about some of these questions:

If I use descriptive language, is it significant?
Do the details of the sculpture make themselves felt?
Am I thinking verse, not prose?
Is the language as spare as possible?
Is the narrative clear?
Do I raise questions that I do not answer?
Have I read the myth aloud, to myself and someone else?
Have I accomplished my purpose?

Conferring is the most useful way to help the children with their revision, especially if they read their myths aloud. I will sometimes show the children what their verse sounds like without the adjectives. Or what it sounds like if we put line breaks in certain places. Or what it sounds like if we incorporate repetition or some archaic phrasing. They may confer with you, and in partnerships, and perhaps in small response groups. Reading their myths aloud in stable response groups helps the students plan and evaluate revision. They need plenty of time to write, and read aloud again, and write again. As they finish, it might be helpful to have a center in the room where students help each other with editing. I also have an editing checklist for the children and usually a rubric as well (see pages 138–39). Since they may all be at different stages in their writing, it is important for them to have some autonomy over these stages.

AFTERTHOUGHTS

When I write down all the possible things we could do in this workshop, I become afraid that someone will want to try them all, and then it feels like there is a lot of teaching in this workshop. You don't need to do everything I have described in this chapter. I have shown some possible ways the workshop could look on pages 132–33. If the children are young, you may want to just tell a few myths, look, and write in the presence of the sculptures. Give the most time for looking and writing. Give the least time to instruction and make most of the instruction happen in side-by-side interactions. The instruction is meant to support the children as writers. It is intended to lift their writing to new levels. But we also know that their writing will move forward in response to the sculptures and to making the classroom a place where we have the freedom to dream. Maintain that space. This is your time to dream mythic dreams. It is a time for transformation.

Transformation may mean different things in our classrooms. It may mean Elai and David daring to write antihomophobic narratives. It may mean a class spending much of its time looking at art. It may mean the intimacy engendered by storytelling. And it may mean transformation of

FIGURE 4–8   *Statuette of a Veiled and Masked Dancer* (detail)

how the children imagine their writing powers. Sixth grader Stephanie, for instance, found writing frustrating, and reading also. She read very slowly and wrote only short pieces, also slowly. She benefited simply from having entry points for writing that started with looking, from instruction that was mostly oral, and from writing in verse. She soaked up everything we said about myth. She looked, she listened, and she did write. Here is Stephanie's myth, inspired by the sculpture *Statuette of a Veiled and Masked Dancer* (see Figure 4–8). It is a hopeful final piece for this book, because it is about joy being maintained in the world.

The Dancer

> In ancient Greece
> people lived in villages
> and walked in the dust
> from place to place
> and worked all day in the fields
> picking olives until their fingers were sore
> and their backs hurt.
> And there was no joy in the world.
>
> The villagers worked
> and walked and ate and slept
> and then they woke
> and did it all over again.
>
> And then one day
> a woman walked into a village
> far above the Aegean.
> She was wrapped in brown veils
> that were tight around her body
> and loose around her feet.
> Even her face, and her hair were veiled,
> all except her eyes
> which were black and snappy.
>
> She wouldn't pick olives
> and she wouldn't walk in the dust
> from place to place
> and she wouldn't lie down at night.
> Instead she danced
> a whirling, twirly dance
> she spun like a top
> and all the villagers looked at her
> at her veils flying out
> and her feet twirling,
> and they wanted to spin too.

As she danced the villagers forgot their work
they forgot the dust
and the olives waiting to be picked
and they danced with her
around and around
laughing and twirling
swirling and whirling
until they fell into their beds laughing.

And from that day
there was joy in the world
and even when the villagers work
all day in the dust
even when their backs hurt
and their fingers are sore
they know there will be a time for dancing
and even as they pick the olives
their feet tap twirly patterns in the dust.

REFERENCES

Butler, J. 1990/1999. *Gender Trouble*. New York: Routledge.

Dewey, J. 1916/1944. *Democracy and Education. An Introduction to the Philosophy of Education*. New York: Free.

Egan, K. 1990. *Romantic Understanding: The Development of Rationality and Imagination, Ages 8–15*. New York: Routledge.

———. 1992. *Imagination in Teaching and Learning: The Middle School Years*. Chicago: University of Chicago Press.

Hamilton, E. 1950. *Mythology*. London: Little, Brown.

Lattimore, R. 1977. *The Iliad*. New York: Harper & Row.

Mandelbaum, A. 1993. *The Metamorphoses of Ovid*. New York: Harcourt Brace.

Mosse, G. 1996. *The Image of Man: The Creation of Modern Masculinity*. New York: Oxford University Press.

Pastan, L. 1982. *PM/AM*. New York: W. W. Norton.

Stafford, W. 1996. *Even in Quiet Places*. Lewiston, ID: Confluence.

Books with Images of Greek Sculpture

Boardman, J. 1985. *Greek Sculpture: The Classical Period*. London: Thames and Hudson.

Smith, R. R. R. 1991. *Hellenistic Sculpture*. London: Thames and Hudson.

Stewart, A. 1990. *Greek Sculpture: An Exploration*. New Haven, CT: Yale University Press.

Online Collections of Greek Sculpture

www.metmuseum.org/   A website for the Metropolitan Museum of Art, New York. If you click on "the collection" you can view highlights of each collection, including fifty images from the Greek and Roman collection. *Statue of an Old Market Woman* is one of these, and there are multiple views of the *Statuette of a Veiled and Masked Dancer*. There is also a lovely *Kouros*, a standing warrior from the archaic period. This website currently allows you to make your own personal Metmuseum collection online, where you can store and access your images.

www.christusrex.org/www1/vaticano/0-Musei.html   The collection, although not the official website, of the Vatican Museum in Rome. Go to "sculpture museum I and II" to view and download superlative images of Greek sculpture. Absolutely the richest collection of images of Greek sculpture I have found online. *The Laocoon* is here, the famous Hellenistic sculpture of Laocoon battling the serpents, and the *Belvedere Apollo* is here as well. The site is not always available, so when it is, download the images you want to a file.

www.museicapitolini.org/en/index_msie.htm   The collection of the Capitoline Museum in Rome. Go to "photographic gallery" to access and download images, including the *Dying Gaul* and others. Click on the time periods named on the time lines, and more images will appear.

www.louvre.fr/   The website for the Louvre Museum in Paris. Click first on "English" then go to "collections." You can look at and download images. There are hoards of glorious ancient sculptures, including *Artemis the Huntress* and the *Nike of Samothrace*.

www.getty.edu/   The website of the Getty collection in Los Angeles. Click on "collections" and then "sculpture" to access this collection, which has some lovely Cycladic figures.

http://harpy.uccs.edu/greek/hellsculpt.html   A website of Hellenistic sculpture, including *The Dying Gaul, The Boxer,* and *The Nike of Samothrace. The Boxer* is a good one for narrative possibilities.

Some Easy-to-Read Material for Learning Centers

Cerasini, M. 1997. *The Twelve Labors of Hercules*. New York: Random House.

Hull, R. E. 2000a. *Entertainment and the Arts*. The World of Ancient Greece series. New York: Franklin Watts.

———. 2000b. *Everyday Life*. The World of Ancient Greece series. New York: Franklin Watts.

———. 2000c. *Religion and the Gods*. The world of ancient Greece series. New York: Franklin Watts.

Little, E. 1988. *The Trojan Horse*. New York: Random House.

McClean, M. 1973. *Adventures of the Greek Heroes*. New York: Houghton Mifflin.

Shuter, J. 1999a. *Builders, Traders, and Craftsmen.* The Ancient Greeks series. Barrington, IL: Heinemann Library.

———. 1999b. *Farmers and Fighters.* The Ancient Greeks series. Barrington, IL: Heinemann Library.

———. 1999c. *Cities and Citizens.* The Ancient Greeks series. Barrington, IL: Heinemann Library.

Afterword

Children take up writing in many ways. For some children, writing becomes their primary form of communicating with the world. For some children, writing becomes a barricade against the world, a way to interpret and reject oppressive experiences. Writing can be a way to reassert control over story lines that have become lost to us or to achieve release from story lines we do not wish to inhabit. So we need to teach writing in ways that enable children to envision and create change through the act of writing. And we do need to see writing as an art, to believe that children's writing has aesthetic potential. For functional writing will only maintain present positions in the world.

I hope that this book shows some ways to teach children about writing that have aesthetic possibilities. To teach writing as a way of coming to know. To teach writing as a means of shifting perspectives. To teach writing so that we write into existence new narratives of love and of transformation. To teach writing as way to care for the world and for each other, and to find things to love in the world and things to hold on to.

Sometimes as teachers we seem to have so many blockades around us. So many standardized tests, and they matter for the children's placement. So much time that is controlled. Such limited access to truly breathtaking resources. So much that is confusing in the world around us. And yet, there is still so much possibility. Possibility remains to create meaningful studies and opportunities within the curricula we inherit. Possibilities remain to have many side-by-side, intimate conversations with children that lead to revelation. Possibilities remain to reflect on the experiences our children have in school and think how we can transform some of these into aesthetic experiences. Experiences that help us cohabit in nourishing ways.

Appendices

A Note on More Images

The images as they are reproduced in the book are, some of them, of a size and clarity that children could look closely and write effectively from these reproductions. Most, however, need to be reproduced in greater size, detail, and color than this publication allows. It matters that the images be clear and as large as possible if we want the children to be able to examine detail and to have intimate, aesthetic experiences that can lead to writing. Please visit the companion website (*www.heinemann.com/ehrenworth*) and download the images in color! Almost all of the images that illustrate the workshops are also available online at the websites listed at the end of the chapters. To download these images, go to the listed website, then click your mouse button on the image, and choose "save picture as" to save it as a file on a hard drive or a disk. You may also copy and insert the images. With either of these methods you may keep the images stored in a picture file, or you can insert them into a document.

To gain access to more images online, you may simply go to Yahoo! and type in categories such as "Ancient Greek sculpture" or "American landscape painting." You may also enter the names of various museums, as many national and international museums have lovely online collections now. Some favorite sites that have gorgeous digital images include the following:

http://arthist.cla.umn.edu/aict/index.html   From the Minneapolis Academy of Art and Design, a free-use image site for teaching college art history, which includes ancient to modern Western and Eastern art. A very rich site.

www.metmuseum.org   The Metropolitan Museum of Art, New York. Ancient to modern art. Enter and go to "collections."

www.louvre.fr/   The Louvre Museum, Paris. Ancient to Impressionist art. Choose "English" and then "collections."

www.getty.edu/   The Getty Museums. Choose collections and you can look at hundreds of individual artists and thousands of paintings, sculptures, and decorative objects.

www.artic.edu/aic/   The Art Institute of Chicago. Not all of the collections are online, but the ones on view are striking. Choose "collections."

www.mfa.org/   The Boston Museum of Fine Arts. Enter and choose "collections."

www.philamuseum.org/   Philadelphia Museum. A small but lovely collection, including Eastern and American art.

Some Support Structures for Writing

Observation Record Sheet—Picasso and Portraiture

Name: _____

Title of Painting: _____

1. How does Picasso portray the woman in this painting? Write down words or phrases that you think of as you look at her and link them to what you see in the painting:

2. Try to describe the forms and colors that shape the woman and what they suggest:

3. How do you imagine the relationship between the painter and this woman?

Benin—Learning Centers

Learning Center One

Context

In Benin, the Oba is the king and the Iyoba is the mother of the king.

Together the Oba and Iyoba care for the kingdom.

When the Oba and Iyoba seek help, they can pray to their ancestors through these sculptures, which are called *altar heads*.

Some altar heads show cultural symbols of power, including coral bead necklaces, scars from ritual scarification, upright posture, a round cap for the Oba, and long braids, or sidelocks.

Some show symbols of beauty, including high cheekbones, large and outlined eyes, long braids, and symmetrical features.

Instructions

Please make a detailed sketch of each of these heads on clean white paper.

Label symbols of power and beauty in each drawing. Note which symbols are common to both heads and which seem to be unique.

Learning Center Two

Context

The altar tusk is a carved elephant tusk that is placed in the hole in the center of the altar head of the Oba.

The purpose of the altar tusk is to show the important accomplishments of this Oba. The carvings may also include spirits and priests who help the Oba as well as enemies he defeats.

The altar rings were possibly worn by sacrificial prisoners or placed on altars.

Symbols of defeat, including beheadings and death, are often carved on these neck rings.

Instructions

On two clean pieces of white paper, please make a small sketch of the tusk and the neck ring. Next to each, make a close-up sketch of one or more figures from each and label who you think the figures are and explain their significance.

Underneath your drawing, please explain in one sentence your theory for the significance of some of the figures on the tusk and the neck ring—why do you think they are included on the tusk or neck ring?

Benin—Learning Centers (continued)

Learning Center Three

CONTEXT

Wooden rattle staffs are rung by priests and the Oba to call good spirits.

Brass altar bells in Benin are rung by Obas to alert the spirits of their ancestors to their prayers.

The mudfish (a catfish) is a sign of good fortune and prosperity in Benin.

INSTRUCTIONS

On two clean pieces of white paper, please make a sketch of each object.

Label and annotate any design on each image that you think may have religious significance.

Culturally Flexible Short Stories

Charting Character-Setting Relationships

SETTING	CHARACTER

Outlining Possible Structures

PURPOSE:
SETTING:
NARRATOR/CHARACTERS:
WHAT HAPPENS:
THE ARTIFACTS:

Looking at Sculpture and Painting

WHAT I SEE	WHAT I THINK	WHAT I WONDER

Possible Planning Schedules for Mythology

Week One	**Week One**
Oral storytelling, "The Old Market Woman"	Looking
Looking at sculptures	Oral storytelling
Reading aloud some myths	**Week Two**
Children freewriting and storytelling	Looking
Week Two	Listening to myths and literary conversation about myths and their purposes
Conversation about purpose and lesson on narrative structure	**Week Three**
Drafting	Learning centers
Week Three	Listening to myths
Peer conferences	**Week Four**
Craft lessons	Looking for detail
Revision	Looking for narrative possibility
	Oral storytelling and freewrites
	Week Five
	Lessons on purpose and structure
	Drafting
	Week Six
	Craft lessons
	Revision
	Week Seven
	Peer conferences
	Revision
	Publishing

An Editing Checklist

Tense

Is it consistent? Is it appropriate? Does it do the work I want it to do? Have I
checked my verb endings to make sure they are working for me?

Punctuation

I have periods where I want my reader to stop.

I have commas, especially where I want my reader to pause.

Have I capitalized the first letter of the first word of a new sentence so my reader
knows I'm moving on?

Have I capitalized names and places so my reader knows those matter?

Do I use question marks when I want the reader to wonder?

Wow! Those exclamation points should just get out of here except in dialogue!

Grammar

Sentence fragments. Make the pace more rapid. That's what they do. Really.

If I use a long run-on sentence that seems like it is never ever ever going to end and just keeps on
going until it is almost a paragraph in length and the reader is running out of breath and starting
to pass out, is it for a reason or is it just because I have abandoned the reader and gone out to
lunch myself while she is stuck in this single sentence from which she may never escape and
may die of hunger while I sit on the floor of my bedroom with my cat and eat pizza with ancho-
vies, pepperonis, and small bits of cut-up Italian sausage?

Do I indent new thoughts, making a new paragraph and telling my reader we are on to something new?

Do I use "quotation marks" to show that someone is speaking aloud?

Style

Have I gotten rid of all those initially appealing, but really rather pesky adjectives?

Are my verbs strong? Do they cut and jab and skitter?

Is there voice? Is it my voice?

The Big Question

Have I read it aloud?

Sample Rubrics for Our Writing

Rubric A

Clarity of purpose, form, structure	20%
Inventiveness	20%
Development of ideas and imagery	20%
Risk taking for you as a writer	20%
Editing and formal conventions	20%

Rubric B (Particularly for Mythology)

Attention to sculptural detail	20%
Incorporation of mythic elements, including imagery, repetition, attributes	20%
Clarity of purpose and structure	20%
Clarity of language	20%
Historical accuracy and flavor	10%
Editing and formal conventions	10%

Additional Historial Background Briefs

Some More on Picasso (1881–1973)

Picasso was an artist for more than seventy years. In some ways, because he was always experimenting and innovating, and in part for his longevity, his work charts the development of modern art. He followed no single style, would be limited by no official school. In his work he searched for the unpredictable. His art is an intensely personal experience that reflects the artist's interaction with the world around him.

Pablo Ruiz Picasso was born in Málaga in 1881. His father was a painter and instructor of art. Picasso passed his entrance examination for the Barcelona School of Fine Art at the age of fifteen without trouble and was swiftly bored with representational painting, which came very easily to him. When he was nineteen, Picasso paid his first visit to Paris with his close friend the painter Casagemus, who was to commit suicide over an unrequited love affair. The death of Casagemus put Picasso into a depression, initiating the melancholy, sentimental Blue Period (1895–1905). The artist was ill and poor. He was lonely. Many of the works from this period show families of traveling performers known as *saltimbanques*, lonely, sad, bathed in a blue light that makes everything melancholic.

Five years later Picasso moved to Paris. He sold a few paintings to the American writer Gertrude Stein and she was to help his early career. In Paris Picasso met Fernande Olivier, and she came to live with him. He also made the acquaintance of the painters Matisse and Braque. At first the characters in his work were still the marginalized and the poor, such as blind beggars, absinthe drinkers, and harlequins. Gradually Paris and his love for Fernande changed his mood, leading to the Rose Period (1905–06). In these paintings he bathes everything in a rosy, rather nostalgic pink wash. In the summer of 1906, Picasso went with his mistress to a small Catalan hill village. Perhaps in response to the sculpted cliffs around him, the faces in his paintings became more stylized and geometric. Picasso's portrait of Gertrude Stein, which is in the Metropolitan Museum of Art, marks the transition to a new period. The sculptural body is still in a classic vein, while the geometric, simplified face and empty eyes prefigure Cubism. The artist claimed that he painted not what she looked like then, but what she would come to look like.

In the spring of 1907, Picasso showed his friends his large and astonishing new proto-Cubist painting, *Les Demoiselles d'Avignon*, which is now in the Museum of Modern Art in New York. His friends recommended that he not continue in this vein and even mourned the loss of a great artist. This work shows the influence of Iberian statuary, African masks, and the germs of Cubism. The forms are geometric, the proportions exaggerated, the colors harsh. The women, in a brothel, stare out at the viewer challengingly. It was a bold and shocking image that challenged traditional ideas of perspective, space, form, and female beauty. Picasso found that Braque had been working in a similar vein in a series of landscapes that earned him the derisive title "cubist." Picasso and Braque began to work closely together, exploring this new style. Cubism for Picasso began with a phase focused on the study of volume, light, and space, fragmenting solid surfaces into facets, very influenced by Cézanne. Following this was the Analytic Cubism phase, in which the figures and shapes were broken down and analyzed. Analytic Cubism was extremely disciplined and formulaic. Objects were looked at simultaneously from several angles. This phase was followed by the Synthetic Cubism phase, in which paintings were built up in layers like collage. Real details such as newspapers and chair caning were introduced. In 1912 Picasso separated from Fernande to take up with Eva, or Ma Jolie, whom he painted in a Cubist portrait of that name.

In 1914 the First World War broke out, putting an end to the collective adventure of Cubism. Braque joined his regiment in August, and most of Picasso's friends joined up or left Paris. World War I took its toll on Picasso's circle. Influenza swept Europe. Eva died in 1915. Two years later, Picasso saw Diaghilev's Ballet Russe, the famous Russian ballet company that was touring Europe. In the company was the ballerina Olga Kokhlova. Picasso married Olga and stayed in Paris except for summers at the seaside.

At the end of the war, Olga and Picasso often visited the seaside at Biarritz and the Côte d'Azur, providing new themes for his work. This stage marked the development of enormous, large-scale women in Picasso's work. Neoclassical forms appeared. A favorite model for Picasso was Sara Murphy, the American expatriate. The postwar climate was intensely nationalist and traditional. In a time when a whole generation had been decimated at war, women were seen as the sign of endurance and rebirth. It was the women who would survive and who would repopulate the earth. The women in these work appear as monumental earth goddesses. In *Women at the Spring*, 1921, in the Museum of Modern Art, New York, three women gather at a spring to collect water. The water rising from the earth to give life is itself a symbol of resurgence, as is the ancient and traditional act of these women. The treatment of the drapery brings to mind classical columns, with the classical ideas of freedom and liberty. These are postwar ideas that comforted decimated nations, gave them the idea that life would begin again and that Europe could be reborn in a better way. In 1921 Olga gave birth to Paolo, who would be much reproduced in Picasso's work. Closely involved in his new family and in the rebirth of a nation, Picasso produced many images of motherhood.

In the late 1920s, Picasso's mood became more fierce and more surrealistic. It is known as his Monster Period. The buildup of fascism in Europe coincided with hostility in his personal life. Clashes with Olga caused signs in his work of aggression and violence toward females. Forms became dismembered, the colors bright and harsh. His work was violent and erotic and often hostile to women. In 1927 Picasso met Marie-Thérèse, who became his model and then his mistress. Picasso deceived Olga about Marie-Thérèse until the model became pregnant with Maïa. At that point Olga was told and would not give Picasso a divorce. Picasso was furious. The immense forms in his paintings underwent organic transformations and permutations of genitalia and mouths, metamorphoses reflecting the conflict in the artist's personal world between Olga and Marie-Thérèse Walters.

The late 1930s were troubled years both politically and personally for Picasso. He was to say that it was the worst period of his life. In 1935 his violent clashes with Olga ended finally in a divorce. Marie-Thérèse Walters gave birth to his daughter Maïa, and the following year Picasso was introduced to the American photographer Dora Maar, with whom he would soon start an affair. In 1936 Franco invaded Spain and civil war broke out between the Republicans (antifascists) and the Loyalists, or Falange (the fascist supporters of Franco). Picasso was intensely supportive of the Republican cause. He was made honorary director of the Prado, a job that proved cumbersome when the Prado became a bomb target and had to disperse its collection.

The civil war in Spain is important in order to understand Picasso's painting *Guernica*. Franco mobilized the church and army to a revolt. Against these conservative fascists were the Republicans— intellectuals, democrats, communists, anarchists, Marxists, republican liberals, church liberals. Spain became the testing ground for World War II, as Italian fascists and German Nazis sent troops and supplies to support Franco. It was an opportunity for the fascists to test their weapons and give experience to their troops. The communist Soviet Union sent supplies to the Republicans, a fact that alienated the British and the United States, who refused to help Spain, even as it became increasingly obvious that the civil war in Spain was merely the prelude to a larger international war. One of the most shocking events of the war was the bombing of the Basque town of Guernica on April 26, 1937. The town was a Republican center for civilians, the seriously wounded, and refugee children. On April 26 three squadrons of German Lüftwaffe planes, flying for Franco, destroyed the town in order to clinically observe the effect on morale of killing civilians. It was the first test for the Germans of the new Nazi theory of total warfare—blitzkrieg. The squadrons, under the command of Wolfem von Richthofen, bombed the town, then strafed it to send people into the buildings. Incendiary bombs were then dropped on these buildings, and low-flying planes strafed the remaining fleeing civilians with machine gun fire. Ten thousand people were killed in the raid, mostly women, elderly civilians, wounded veterans, and children. News of the massacre reached the rest of the world through George Steer's article in the *New York Times* of April 27, 1937. This event helped focus support for the Republicans and reveal fascist terrorism.

As the fighting in Spain continued, Picasso's canvases became increasingly violent, culminating in *Guernica*, 1937. This work depicts the bombing of Guernica. It shows the mangled forms of women and children, trampled, fleeing, dying. Flames are seen in the background, the walls cave in. The figures are deliberately distorted to symbolize their physical and spiritual torture. A horse, the symbol of the Spanish people, rears its head in pain and tries to rise, while a bull, the symbol of Franco and the fascists, looks on impassively. The single symbol of hope is the woman entering, holding a light that illuminates the scene. She exposes the truth of the event and the struggle of the Spanish people, just as Picasso's painting also exposes this event. The painting is done in the shades of gray, white, and black, which echo the colors of the newsprint that brought knowledge of this massacre to the world. *Guernica* was displayed first at the Spanish Pavilion of the Paris World Fair in 1937, and then in London, Manchester, and eventually New York. Of *Guernica*, Picasso said: "Painting is not interior decoration. It is an instrument of war, for attack and defense against the enemy." This painting marked the moment of most direct and intense intervention in political affairs for the artist. Perhaps because the fascists won this war, plunging the world into the even larger battles of World War II, the artist was never again to involve his art so intensely in political affairs.

When the Second World War broke out in 1939, Picasso was staying with Dora Maar in Antibes. He spent the rest of the war in Paris, ignoring the bribes of the Germans to support their cause. The privation, butchery, and inhumanity of this second war left a mark on Picasso's work as the first did not. The human form became distorted in his work, cannibalism appeared, forms were tortured. After the liberation of Paris in 1944, Picasso joined the Communist Party. At this time Picasso met Françoise Gilot, who was to bear him Claude and Paloma. In Antibes, Picasso began to work on ceramics.

The early 1950s saw several important events for Picasso—the death of Matisse in 1954, the departure of Françoise Gilot, and the appearance of Jacqueline Roque, whom he married in 1961. In 1955 the artist moved to La Californie, a villa in Cannes. He bought a seventeenth-century palatial chateau in the mountains of Vauvenargues. Picasso worked on homages to Matisse as well as versions of old and modern masters. Toward the end of his life, Spanish themes reentered Picasso's work. He seemed to be interpreting his work through grand personal and artistic epochs. He remained with Jacqueline until his death in 1973.

References

Chipp, H. 1992. *Picasso's Guernica: Histories, Transformations, Meanings.* Berkeley: University of California Press.

Rubin, W., ed. 1996. *Picasso and Portraiture.* New York: Museum of Modern Art.

Some More on Benin

Benin is one of West Africa's most ancient surviving kingdoms, located in the tropical rain forests of southwestern Nigeria. The history of Benin is known from circa 1400, and it is a history of a strong nation organized around central rule. The people are commonly known as *Edo*, as is the language. The king of Benin, who is thought to be divine, is called the *Oba*. The queen mother is called the *Iyoba*. (The mother of the king is the Iyoba, not his wife or wives.) The capital city is Benin City, which is the religious and political center of Benin and the home of the Oba. The rest of Benin is divided into *fiefs* (individual provinces, each ruled by an appointed official). The city is the center of bureaucracy and export, which traditionally was mostly slaves and ivory. Outside of the city, people live in rural farming villages and mostly grow yams, timber, and rubber. The *edion*, or elders, govern the village. The highest authority in the village is the *odionwere*, or oldest man. Occasionally a village will also have a royal family member, known as the *onigie*, as a ruler. Villages will send livestock, food, and soldiers to the capital as tribute. The villages are controlled from the capital by being divided into the tribal fiefs.

Division of rank and power in Benin reflects the central authority of the Oba. He is the supreme religious figure, a god himself with absolute power over his people. The Oba is believed to be descended from a divinity and to be divine. He is not supposed to need to eat or sleep, and the well-being of the kingdom resides in him. Through the Oba's ability to channel the spirits of his ancestors, the Edo are protected. Many rituals are performed to bring the Oba closer to his ancestors and to reinforce his divinity. Besides speaking with his ancestors and the gods, the Oba also controls all trade in Benin, as well as all political appointments and the judicial system. He is *omnipotent*, or all powerful, within Benin, like the ancient Egyptian pharaohs. He is known to his people as the Child of the Sky and Earth, and a Brother to the Sea. The Iyoba is also believed to have supernatural powers, which she can use to help her son the king. An Oba has many wives. The first one to grant him a healthy son may be proclaimed Iyoba, or queen mother, after her son has been crowned king (hence, after her husband dies). The Iyoba fills the only position of political power for females in Benin.

The Oba is helped in administering his kingdom by three chief groups. The highest of these is the *uzama*, who are priest-nobles who perform religious rituals that protect the king and the kingdom. According to Benin history, the uzama lived in Benin even before the Oba, and they chose the first Oba. Thus, they sometimes think themselves more powerful than the Oba, resulting in political and religious conflicts. There are seven uzama, including in their ranks a guardian of the most important shrine in Benin, the crown prince, and two military commanders. The second group is the *palace chiefs*, aristocrats who administer the government, trade, and the king's everyday affairs. The third group is the *town chiefs*, who collect tribute from the villages, recruit the military, and are involved in village administration. Among the highest ranking of the town chiefs is the *iyase*, who is one of the supreme military commanders, not apparently always faithful to the Oba. These three groups administer the kingdom, and their intergroup struggles for power help maintain a balance of power in Benin.

The royal art of Benin, made primarily of carved ivory and cast brass, glorifies the king and his court. He controls the artists guilds, and art and costume in Benin are deliberately designed to reinforce the power and mystery of the Oba. Elaborate costumes are designed for the Oba, with royal coral beads as decoration. He is also the only one to wear the *ada* sword of ceremonial power. On a mud altar are placed several objects, the most important of which are the altar heads of the Oba's ancestors. It is the Oba's altar heads which are seen to protect and guide the kingdom. These altar heads, made of cast brass, show the Obas in their coral bead necklaces, with their beaded cap crown, long sidelocks, and often three ritual scars above the eyes. Through these heads, the Oba can communicate with ancestors. Each head supports a large carved ivory tusk. The figures on these tusks, read from the bottom to the top, show achievements of past Obas and sources of the Obas' power. Heads of the Iyoba have a high beak hairstyle, which is worn only by noble Edo women, a coral bead crown and coral bead necklaces, and often four ritual scars above the eyes. The right to wear a coral bead crown is limited to the Oba, the Iyoba, and the war chief. With the exception of a few sixteenth-century heads, altar heads are not naturalistic. They are idealized to emphasize the symbols of power (necklaces, crown, scars, and posture) and beauty (high cheekbones, full lips, exaggerated eyes).

In the center of the altar is an altar tableau of several figures, often showing the Oba or Iyoba involved in a ceremony. Near or on the altar will also be wooden rattle staffs, used to summon ancestor spirits, and altar bells, used to call spirits and frighten enemies. Brass figures of animals, particularly leopards and roosters, also decorate the altars. Other brass objects include neck rings, perhaps worn by captives in human sacrifices, and brass plaques which decorated the wall of the royal palace. These altars, objects, and costumes are still used in Benin today, to affirm the power and divinity of the present Oba.

There are many important rituals in Benin tradition, some of them incorporating human or animal sacrifices, and all of them involving royal art and ritual objects. These palace rituals and sacrifices take place following the planting of the crops and the harvest, as well as in periods of war. Most ritual objects of Benin are made of ivory or brass, with the exception of the wooden carved stools used in palace ceremonies and the wooden rattle staffs. One of the most important rituals is called *Ugie Erha Oba*. In Ugie Erha Oba, which honors the king and his ancestors, all his priests first clear a path for him with magic bracelets. Animal and human sacrifices are then performed to appease evil spirits and to honor the earth and the Oba's ancestors. Then the chiefs dance past the Oba with raised ceremonial swords. The ritual concludes with a mock battle between the king and the nobles. This battle is won by the king, reinforcing his power. In a second ritual, *Igue*, the chiefs and nobles confirm their loyalty to the Oba and acknowledge the Oba's divinity. In this ritual the Oba absorbs medicines, and then both tame and wild animals such as cows and leopards are sacrificed. The rite ends when children rush out of the capital, carrying torches to drive away evil spirits. In both rituals, rattle staffs are shaken to call spirits.

Artistic and religious tradition in Benin has continued since the fifteenth century with only one major interruption due to European interference. The Benin first came into contact with Europeans when Portuguese traders came across the sea in the fifteenth century to purchase slaves. The Portuguese also tried to convert the Benin by converting the Oba and his son to Christianity, but they had little success beyond introducing their new god into the polytheism of Benin. Besides acting as traders and missionaries, the Portuguese served as mercenaries (professional soldiers) in the Benin army, and they introduced firearms. In Benin art the Portuguese are depicted with beards, mustaches, long hair, sharp noses, and European dress. Later, the Dutch and English traded with Benin, until the nineteenth century, when a British trade expedition, proceeding into Benin City against the wishes of the Oba during a religious ceremony, was massacred. The British then sent a military force, known as the Benin Punitive Expedition, to capture and destroy Benin City in 1897. Afterward the British controlled Benin, put an end to human sacrifices, and allowed the Oba only ceremonial powers. The Oba went into exile until 1914, when he regained his position as leader of the Republic of Benin, within the state of Nigeria. The present Oba traces his lineage back to that of his royal fifteenth-century ancestors in an unbroken line.

Reference

Ezra, K. 1992. *Royal Art of Benin: The Perls Collection*. New York: Metropolitan Museum of Art and Harry M. Abrams.

Some Student Writing

Poetry and Portraiture

Bather with Beach Ball

I want to bounce on the beach
like a ball
across the sand
with the ocean behind me
and the blue, blue sky
your hair will blow
and I will blow kisses
come bounce with me
and bring sand into the house

Nelson, grade five

Benin Short Stories

The Mud Altar

Long ago in Africa, in West Africa, there was a boy who was born in a muddy village. He was poor. His family was poor. He had a sister and she was poor and muddy. They were muddy all the time. They lived in small huts and the mud came inside. It got in their clothes and their food. No-one knew what to do with so much mud.

One day, the Oba visited the village. He was king of all Benin. He wore necklaces around his neck of orange beads. He had scars on his forehead to show he was brave. His hair was in long braids to show he was strong. Oba stayed the night in the village and the village put him in a hut. He got very muddy.

Oba wanted to pray to his father, who was dead and was now a god-spirit. He had the brass head so he could speak to his father. He had the tusk that showed his father as Oba. But he had nowhere to put them. He put them down in the mud and cried.

The boy was outside the hut sitting in the mud. He heard Oba cry and he came inside. He asked Oba what was wrong. Oba said "I don't have anywhere to put the head of my father." The boy said "I will help you." He sat in the mud and he made a table out of the mud. The Oba put his father's head on the table and he was happy.

This is a story about why the altars in Benin are made out of mud. And it also shows how we should make the best of things.

Willie, grade three

Mythology

The Dancer

In ancient Greece
people lived in villages
and walked in the dust
from place to place
and worked all day in the fields
picking olives until their fingers were sore
and their backs hurt.
And there was no joy in the world.

The villagers worked
and walked and ate and slept
and then they woke
and did it all over again.

And then one day
a woman walked into a village
far above the Aegean.
She was wrapped in brown veils
that were tight around her body
and loose around her feet.
Even her face, and her hair were veiled,
all except her eyes
which were black and snappy.

She wouldn't pick olives
and she wouldn't walk in the dust
from place to place
and she wouldn't lie down at night.
Instead she danced
a whirling, twirly dance
she spun like a top
and all the villagers looked at her
at her veils flying out
and her feet twirling,
and they wanted to spin too.

As she danced the villagers forgot their work
they forgot the dust
and the olives waiting to be picked
and they danced with her
around and around
laughing and twirling
swirling and whirling
until they fell into their beds laughing.

And from that day
there was joy in the world
and even when the villagers work
all day in the dust
even when their backs hurt
and their fingers are sore
they know there will be a time for dancing
and even as they pick the olives
their feet tap twirly patterns in the dust.

Stephanie, grade six

Alexander and Diomedes
(The Dying Warrior)

From the age of five Alexander and Diomedes
trained together in the gymnasium
with the long spears
and with iron swords.
They swore they would never betray one
      another
never swerve in battle
never abandon the other in life or in love
or in death.

At sixteen they left the gymnasium to take up
      their lives
Diomedes became a breeder of horses
and Alexander trained them
as their fathers had before them
and their fathers' fathers.

But war came
and they left the horses in the green fields
and took up their long spears
and their iron swords
and they prayed to great-hearted Ares
to give them courage.

Alexander and Diomedes stood together
as the Gauls poured out of the forests
their faces painted and their bodies also,
silver torques marking their leaders.

Alexander brought down a Gaul
not much older than Diomedes,
and a bit like him except for the paint.
The wounded youth lay gasping in the dirt,
pushing himself up with one hand
a hole in his side where the sword had gone
      through.
Alexander thought to help him up
and then remembered, he was there to kill him.

The Gauls kept coming,
the air rang with war cries.
Back to back the two boys fought

Each protecting the other
Iron swords clashing
Calling only to each other
Until Apollo, the lord who strikes from afar
jealous of this devotion,
guided the iron-tipped spear of a Gaul
to the tender place above Diomedes's heart
and Apollo's javelin entered also
and Diomedes fell in the dust.

Alexander stood over Diomedes's body
and looked at it with love and horror.
Where was the wound?
And then he saw the blood seeping from
      beneath the armor.
A javelin must have pierced him
under the arm where the leather parted.
They taught the Gauls to look for the place.

He stood over the body
and decided that he would not leave this spot.
And he raised his sword calmly
to face the enemy rushing toward him.
He brought ten of them with him into the dark
And since that day
the Greeks save the Sacred Band, the legion of
      warrior-lovers
for their most desperate defenses
not because they are the most skilled warriors
but because they know the meaning of honor.

Elai, grade eight

Some Interactive Writing

Picasso and Poetry

If Picasso Were Here, on September 11

(a poem inspired by *El Guernica*, 1937, and the events of
September 11, 2001, New York City)

If Picasso were here,
would he put the planes in his painting?
Pushing into the buildings like play-dough,
so silent on the television,
silent as the buildings falling
like tinker-toys or Lego blocks on those tiny
   screens.
But we felt them like an earthquake
   under us.
The school rocked
and the air turned gray
and we didn't know which way to run.

If Picasso were here,
would he put the firemen in,
holding up their lights
like moonbeams in the dark hallways?
Like the light in his painting,
that light bulb blazing with hope,
with truth and courage in a darkened world.

Would he paint the people jumping
from the high windows?
Or the people stepping over them?
Or the people on fire?
Or would he just show the city watching
and the children crying,
and that would be enough?

And does that light keep burning
even though they lost that Civil War in Spain,
the one he painted the painting about,
and we are, (we think), dropping bombs
   right now,
someplace in Afghanistan?
And if it is burning, can we see it?
Because we don't feel safe anymore
and we need someone to paint that light.

*Class 600 in collaboration
with Mary Ehrenworth*

Some Writing for Children

Benin Short Story

The False Bride

Once in a village by a river in Benin twin girls were born five minutes apart and identical in face and body. The girls were known as Elder Sister and Younger Sister. By the time they were twelve the girls wore their hair in dark braids down to their waist. They had bright eyes. They had soft voices. They danced gracefully and when they danced their feet made magic, their voices wove songs, and the beads in their hair rung like bells.

One night the girls were asked to dance for visitors from the palace. In the flickering light of many torches, their feet made intricate patterns in the dust. Their long hair swirled around them, and their voices made soft melodies and harmonies against the dark. When Elder Sister and Younger Sister danced, it seemed like the world would always be a place for dancing and for singing and for love. A leopard came from the edge of the jungle to watch. Crocodiles crawled out of the river to listen. Birds stopped their cries so that they could hear the voices of the girls singing. Even the river moved more slowly, pausing to listen to the girls and watch them dance.

Elder Sister and Younger Sister were judged to be pleasing by the palace officials, and both girls were chosen to be brides to the Oba. Oba was a young king still. He had several brides, but none yet to whom he had given his heart, and none yet who had borne him a son.

Elder Sister and Younger Sister took a vow to always be true to one another. By the river they clasped hands.

"I will be true to you beyond all others, sister dear," said Younger Sister.

"I too," said Elder Sister. "In the palace as in the village, always I will know that I have my sister to trust and to care for me, and I shall care for her and love her always."

On the day before the betrothal the girls went to the river to bathe. Elder Sister, whose heart was gentle, leaned over the river to gather water. The rains had been falling for many days, and seeing the force of the water, she turned.

"Younger Sister," she said. "See how the water tumbles from the recent rains. Surely we shall be washed away."

"Oh beloved sister," Younger Sister replied. "Hold my hand as you lean over the water, and I will keep you safe."

But when Elder Sister leaned out over the river, Younger Sister, whose heart was small and hard, pushed her into the river. The waters closed over the head of Elder

Sister. Younger Sister tore at her clothes and her hair and rolled in the mud. She returned to the village and cried out that Elder Sister had fallen in the river and drowned, and that she had not been able to save her, although she had tried. All the village comforted Younger Sister.

Alone, Younger Sister became the youngest bride of the Oba. She put her hair up in a cone. Oba called her beloved and she became the most favored of all wives. She wore many coral bead necklaces, and she wore beads in her hair also, and she was called First Wife, and not Younger Sister anymore.

The first year that First Wife came to live in the palace, the rain stopped falling in the kingdom of Benin. The Oba called together his priests, and they consulted the ancestor spirits. They rung the brass altar bells to alert the spirits, and shook the wooden rattle staffs to summon their assistance.

Still the rains did not come. The rivers dried up and the mudfish lay on the surface of the mud and died. The fruits fell hard and bitter from the branches of dying trees. There was no water to grow things and none for the animals. There was no water for children, or for the old, and hunger and death and great suffering came to Benin.

At the palace Oba knelt in front of the mud altar where the brass heads of his ancestors sat. He called to the spirit of his grandfather to explain why Benin suffered, why the people and the animals and the land were without water for so long. Oba heard no words, but as he looked into the staring eyes of the altar head of his grandfather, he saw a vision. He saw First Wife as a village girl. She held Elder Sister's hand as she leaned into the river, and then she let go. He saw Elder Sister hit her head on a rock, and float down the river, and he saw Younger Sister return to the village and dress in her wedding finery. Oba saw no more, but he knew, now, that the rains had stopped because he had welcomed evil into the palace.

Oba summoned First Wife. He stripped her of her coral bead necklaces.

He said, "You are no longer First Wife. You shall be known as Evil Sister, and all shall turn from you."

And Oba put an altar ring on Evil Sister's neck and sent her out from the palace. The neck ring had carvings on it of figures whose heads had been chopped off, who were being eaten by vultures, to show the death that Evil Sister had brought to Benin. She could not remove the ring, and without her necklaces, she could not hide it. Evil Sister let her hair down to cover the ring, and went into the jungle.

And yet still no rain fell.

Oba thought then that the gods needed him to make a sacrifice. To protect his people he decided to sacrifice Evil Sister, who had shown herself to be an enemy of all. He sent searchers out from the palace to find her.

The priests searched for many days. Days through which no rain fell. They searched in the jungle and in the villages and along the dried-up river where the people still sought water, and down by the sea.

The priests returned after many months with a young woman they had found where the river met the sea. She wore no neck ring, but her face was that of First Wife. This woman had an old wound on her head, and she claimed not to know Oba. Yet Oba prepared with the priests to sacrifice the young woman. They brought her into the palace to prepare her. Even as they entered the palace, however, the skies filled with clouds and the rains began to fall on Benin, and so they put away their weapons, and the woman lived while they celebrated.

Oba prayed to the oldest Oba again to ask what to do with this woman. He rung the altar bells, and he shook the rattle staffs, and he knelt before the altar head and tusk of his grandfathers. And as he prayed to the ancestor heads, he understood what he could not see on his own—that this woman the priests had brought to the palace was Elder Sister, who had survived the river, and been washed down many days' journey to where the river met the sea.

Oba made Elder Sister his wife. He gave her many coral bead necklaces, and he favored her above all other wives, and the rains came every year. Evil Sister wore the neck ring all her days. Wherever she went the waters dried up, and the vultures came, and she was shunned for causing so much unhappiness with her deceit.

Elder Sister remembered how she was saved, and she made sure that Oba always cared for the ancestor heads. She would not call herself First Wife, but instead called herself She Who Was Taken and Mistaken for First Wife . . . perhaps as a reminder that things are not always what they seem.

Mary Ehrenworth

A Mythology of Artemis in Three Parts

ARTEMIS DREAMT

In the time of Aeschylus and Sophocles, Euripedes and the long-dead Homer, the bards would visit the villages and towns of Greece to tell the stories of the Greek gods and the tales of the heroes. We remember their stories from the versions that were written later, and from the sculptures and temples, paintings and vases that survive. They told of Zeus the omnipotent, and of Achilles the champion, and of the long-fought battle for Troy. But the tales they told were a male history, told by poets and playwrights who spoke for generations of men. I like to imagine, though, that there were female bards who told the forgotten histories of the goddesses and the women of Greece. To these women, Zeus was a faithless consort, and Achilles a sulky child. They told the female tales, and these tales were dark at times, cautionary tales for this world of men.

Such a story is this, told by a female bard. It is a story of love and desire, death and betrayal, vengeance and loss. It is the story of the most female of the Olympian immortals, who asked Zeus to let her remain ever a maiden and not be forced into marriage, Artemis the huntress, goddess of the moon.

The Source[1]

She was born of black-browed Zeus and Leto of the lovely hair
a day before her brother Apollo,
so she could assist Leto with his birth.
Twin children with silver bows.
Artemis of the falling arrows,
Apollo who strikes from afar.
They took a vow to be true to each other
and so they were
entwined on the mountain
Artemis of the evening moon
Apollo of the rising sun
the archers
incandescent in ardor on dark-clouded Olympos.
But Artemis guarded her maidenhead
even from her shining brother
and Apollo sought the pale compliance of earthly maidens
ever pursuing the shielded chasteness of his sister.
Looking darkly at her twin, Artemis of the falling arrows
turned from men, and stepped alone into the forest.
She became the huntress, a guardian of wild beasts
and the virgins who made sacrifices to her.
Dressed in moonlight and pearls
she gathered a band of nymphs and maidens
and reveled with them in secluded streams and sacred groves.
Still she hunted alone, with her swift-footed dogs
Artemis of the silver bow and the white arms, and the heart divided   within
    her
since its split from shining-eyed Apollo.

---

[1] The birth of Artemis is related by Edith Hamilton in her *Mythology* (London: Little, Brown, 1950), p. 434. Hamilton also hints at the great cruelty of which Artemis became capable, without being able to explain its source. The common attributes of Apollo and Artemis are mentioned in the *Iliad*. This poem attempts to emulate the metaphoric language found in the *Iliad*, and to suggest a relationship between Apollo and Artemis as a subtext that will color this multigenre exploration.

A Mythology of Artemis in Three Parts *(continued)*

The bard's voice slowed as she finished her first verse.

"Bring me some wine," she croaked. "There is more to tell. There is Orion, favored by Artemis above all others, until he incites the envy of Apollo and is killed. Though she willed it, death would not come for Artemis upon the loss of her lover. And so she raised his body to the heavens, so that at night he would look down upon her, and she would be less alone. And Artemis swore to avenge the death of Orion, and she watched her brother with careful hatred. Apollo guarded himself against her, until he too loved a mortal, the beautiful Hyacinth. This youth became so beloved of Apollo that the god lived only to please him, and Apollo forgot the wrath of his sister. But she did not forget, and when Apollo and Hyacinth were throwing the discus in jesting competition, she guided Apollo's discus to a mortal blow against young Hyacinth, so that he sank to the ground in death, and Apollo cried out in desperate grief. And Artemis watched tearless, and walked away in silence."[2]

---

[2] Sources vary as to who guided the discus that killed Hyacinth, but most agree that it was a jealous rival of Apollo. Out of his blood Apollo made the flower hyacinth grow. The tale is told in Ovid, *Metamorphoses*, x, 155–218, and retold in Hamilton and in *Bulfinch's Mythology* (New York: Modern Library, 1998).

A Poem for Two Voices[3]

Artemis	*Apollo*
The Death of Orion	The Death of Hyacinth
I saw him first in the	**I saw him first in the**
woods	training grounds
He was	**He was**
hunting	wrestling
His hair was	**His hair was**
long and brown	short and fair
tied back with a leather thong	pushed off his forehead with a band
His skin was	**His skin was**
rough	smooth
and sunburnt	and golden
I watched him	**I watched him**
for nights	for days
Until I knew	**Until I knew**
the sounds he made while sleeping	the way he moved
While he slept I	**While he slept I**
touched his lashes with my tongue	brushed my fingers over his chest
One night he awakened	**One night he awakened**
and pulled me down beside him	and stood swiftly over me
and looked at me with love	**and looked at me with love**

---

[3] For the reader unfamiliar with poems for two voices, the two parts are read simultaneously, with the verses on the same line being read aloud by both readers (marked here in bold). Each reader then reads the next consecutive line, and is silent when there are no words on the next line.

I loved to touch the bones of his hips
 and the skin of **his pelvis**

When

did you decide to take him from me?

We were hunting in the woods

  with the bow

It was a contest

I hadn't yet decided if

I would let him win

He turned to look at me

His face full
  of laughter

But you guided
  my arrow

From the heat of your spirit

It entered through his side
  and quivered in his lung

He cried **my name**
as he died

. . . . **his pelvis**,
his hands, the back of his neck
where the hair curled

Why

did you decide to take him from me?
We were training on the fields

Playing with the discus

It was a contest

I had decided that

I would let him win

He sparkled as he ran

His face full

  of love

But you guided

  my discus

From the coldness of your heart

It struck in the forehead and the
  blood poured down

. . . . **my name** was on his lips
as he died

I couldn't die

                                                 I wanted to die

I made him   **I made him**

                                              a flower

     a belt of stars

    I wish **I could hate you**   . . . . **I could hate you**

    The voice of the bard was tired now, but she had one more tale to tell. It was a new myth, perhaps of her creation, for it was not a myth of heroes and gods, men's illusions as told by the ancient bards.

    "Artemis brought me this tale in a dream, of a child who loved Artemis and lost herself between the goddess and her brother. And that you may know it is true, you may see the proof of the fable carved in marble. So listen now, for this is the final tale tonight."

The Old Market Woman[4]

On a mountaintop high above the Aegean
a girl dances in the moonlight.
Thalia of the flowing hair and graceful limbs.
Her hair is a cloud loose about her body.
Her eyes black in her pale face.
Her hands dart like birds about her.
She offers her body to Artemis of the silver bow,
goddess of the moon.
Her prayers are poems to a passion shared since childhood.

Oh virgin moon who bathes my limbs
Accept my gifts, forgive my sins
Artemisia my adored
beloved goddess, only lord

oh sister may I find you still
hunting love upon the hill
teach me to render in your tongue
the songs of ardor you have sung

The girl dances alone in the small clearing.
Her feet make intricate patterns in the dust.
Her slender limbs sway like young birches.
The moon blankets her in cool shadow
so that she is hidden from all else.
At last she bends backward
the white light caresses her,
she says farewell to her sister,
Artemis of the moon and the silver bow.

Oh sister how I still recall
the dark embrace behind the wall
pools of light behind your eyes
the voice of love where shadows lie

---

[4] This story is an invented myth inspired by the sculpture in the Metropolitan Museum of Art, New York, of the *Statue of an Old Market Woman*, circa 150 B.C.E., marble. It follows the tradition within Greek mythology of explaining the existence of beings and objects, as well as the form of the morality tale.

you pierce the heart in a virgin soul
fragment me yet keep me whole
oh faithful I shall ever be
to hill and moon and you and me

The girl picks up her shift,
her unbound hair a river behind her.
Like a goat she climbs down the mountain
to the white house on the edge of the cliff
where her mother waits alone and
the Aegean ripples darkly far below.

In the one room on the side of the mountain, the
fire burns brightly as the woman feeds the girl
bread and honey and watered wine.
Two beds are cut into alcoves in the wall,
two windows look out, to the sea in front and the mountain behind.
In the tiny yard grow olives and figs,
meager vegetables, and three hungry sheep.

With daybreak the woman is at her wheel
spinning the wool for her loom.
Cloth as sheer as mist,
clothing her daughter in the fabric of the moon.

Thalia leads her sheep to the top of the mountain,
where she dances in the clearing,
readying herself for the moon, and ravishment.
For Phoebus Apollo, the sun god
who fills her clearing with hot light,
she has nothing.
No thoughts, no prayers, no dances.
She offers herself to a virgin goddess,
Artemis of the falling arrows, who scorns men,
who sojourns with Thalia in her white light at darkness,
and leaves her yet undefiled.

My sister do you remember still
the wild dance upon the hill
the silent calling and the chase
the long and liquid loose embrace

So in the glory of her youth, Thalia glitters
on the mountain, bright in the sun of Phoebus Apollo,
the ancient twin and soul-mate of Artemis.
She calls down the gaze of the god like
an arrow to its mark, and she does not know
that he comes behind.
Apollo comes in his pride and his beauty,
outshining the moon in his brightness,
his long limbs slender and strong,
his flesh crackling with desire.
Apollo, lord who strikes from afar,
whose thwarted passion left Daphne a tree,
who flayed Marsyas for his rivalry,
who will not be denied.

He pulls the trembling child to him,
"Thalia of the flowing hair and graceful limbs,
lie with me now in the sunlight, and henceforth be mine."
But the girl is not swayed by his words.
"I desire no man, and the light of the moon is
the only brightness I need,"
Thalia cries and she runs from the hot clearing
to the shelter of her mother's arms
and the white house.
At night she does not seek the mountaintop, but looks
out the small window toward the sea and cries out her fears.

Oh Artemis, my sister moon
I face a most forbidding doom
do not forsake me to my fate
or with your brother I must mate

But Apollo's voice ascends higher than the girl's,
calling out to his sister Artemis to remember their ancient incandescent
    union,
and the promises of loyalty made with it.

Oh sister mine remember now
the words of praise, the whispered vow
this moon-white girl shall be in lieu
I'll lie with her but think of you

In answer white-clad Artemis makes a covenant with her brother
unknown to the girl huddled in the small room.
"You have not earned this girl as you did me Apollo,
and I will not witness her violation. You have tried her once.
If by the third offer you have not won her,
then she is mine.
If she falters and forsakes me, then she is yours
to do with as you will."

With daybreak Apollo appears again in the clearing,
shining-eyed, eager as a boy.
"Thalia, I bring you pearls and gold,
rubies, emeralds, wealth untold."

"Riches hold no charm for me,
so leave me now, and let me be,"
says the girl
and she brushes his hand from her arm,
stepping around him as around her sheep.

Now Apollo's brow darkens at the girl's scorn.
His love becomes tainted with pride.
His heart hardens within him.
When next he meets her in the clearing,
he has his gift ready, Apollo the god who strikes from afar.

Thalia if you lie with me
immortal you shall ever be
Eternal life will be your gift
If to me your lips you lift

Thalia hears his words with awe
her heart shifts within her
and she kneels before him.
In her mind she sends a silent message to Artemis.

Oh sister do you still recall
the moonlit hunt behind the wall
now shall my love in sunlight be
I'll lie with him but think of thee

Thalia lies with Apollo in the sunlit clearing.
And though she longs at first for the cool embraces of his sister,
she comes to crave the days which pass in burning abandon
entwined on the mountaintop.
She finds great joy with the god
and her ardor grows to match his.
But what is a moment for them
is a lifetime for mortals.

Thalia thinks finally of her mother
alone in the house with her loom,
waiting for her daughter to return,
watching the rise of the sun and the moon.
She dashes down the mountain
to the house on the cliff.
She ducks into the room crying
"Mother my mother here I am mother."

Silence
and dust
and an empty chair.

She runs out to the yard where the vegetables grew.
"Oh mother my mother where are you mother?"

Weeds
and stillness
and a small stone with her mother's name.
The date on the grave marker is worn
but she can read that her days of love on the mountain
were years in this house
and her mother's death was a lonely one.

The girl in her anguish cries out to the moon

Oh sister don't forsake me now
but loose me from your brother's vow
This love was at too high a cost
My mother dead, the past now lost

But Artemis' heart is cold and she answers not
and time continues to flow past the girl.
She climbs back to the mountaintop
and the days pass
and her sorrow fades in the light of the clearing
and the bright gaze of her lover,
and Thalia takes pleasure again with Apollo.

Apollo too enjoys the girl
but the softness of his gaze
hides the hardness in his heart
that never melted when she scorned him.
And one day as he twines her hair he holds
it gently up before her eyes,
so that she sees the gray seeping in,
and he looks down the mountain to the village far below,
and she sees through his eyes the slender
limbs of the girls, the smoothness of their skin,
and she sees that she is no longer young
and that love is fled.

She turns to Apollo and his shining eyes mock her.

"You should have questioned this gift twice
eternal life, but at a price
youth and beauty nevermore
endless pain shall now be yours."

Looking beyond her to the young girls at play
the god steps around her, as around her sheep.

Thalia moves down to the house on the cliff.
She spins her wool and works the loom
and takes her trade to the village,
where she knows no one,
they slip away so quickly.
The years pass and others die
but she lives on
in the white house above the Aegean.

Her fingers lose their nimbleness.
Her limbs lose their grace.
Dogs snap and children cry when she passes.
She becomes bent like a willow
and each step brings pain,
until she cannot leave the room
and her eyes see neither day nor night
and she cries out to her sister to set her free.

Oh sister if you still recall
the entwined limbs, the moonlit wall
Release my body from this cave
and send it grateful to the grave.

Artemis of the silver bow
beholds the sagging breasts, the loose teeth,
the ravaged skin of the girl who danced on the mountain.
But the goddess is faithful to her brother and she answers not
and the years pass on.

Thalia pulls herself to the edge of the cliff
and hears the roar of the Aegean far below.
She steps over the edge
falling onto the sharp rocks which tear her skin and pierce her limbs.
Her arms shatter at the sockets.
Her nose cracks off in clumps.
Her features crush down to the bone.
But life does not end.

The villagers pull her armless body out of the sea,
they lead her sightless up the path
back to the house on the cliff.
The years pass on.
No food passes her lips.
Her skin hangs in furrows from her tortured frame.
Her eyes see no light and her ears hear no sound
and still she lives on.
In her mind she makes the prayers that her lipless
mouth cannot whisper.

Oh cruel and wanton gods above
To hide the truth behind your love
Far harsher are the games you play
Than we base mortals may engage

Oh sister do you remember still
the call, the chase upon the hill
'twas you who trapped me by the wall
oh sister do you still recall

oh brother won't you see me still
the child dancing on the hill
'twas you who brought me to the sun
taught me to love ere day was done

but love forgot is like the tide
it lingers not and will not bide
your moon and sun have left me blind
to rot forever on the vine

Now Artemis is moved to pity.
She calls to her brother Apollo to lift his curse,
reminding him of the girl on the mountain
and his days of love in the clearing.
Apollo looks at the
woman rotting on the cliff,
blind and deaf and toothless
and he sees that his vengeance is felt.
"Do with her as you will sister, but you may
not give her back her youth."
And he releases the woman back to Artemis.

Artemis breathes a cold breath into the woman
so that her limbs turn to stone, and her heart stops in her chest
and she pauses there at last
white and cold
above the dark Aegean.

My sister yes I do recall
the long embrace behind the wall
the tangled limbs, the loss of will
oh sister I remember still

Acknowledgments

I want to acknowledge first the teachers and children of New York City, with whom I have passed so much time, in such delightful ways. Even in times of budget crisis, times of terror and fear, times of increased testing and great pressure to perform in particular ways, teachers hold on to the things they believe in and create opportunities for their students to learn in joyful and lasting ways.

So much of the thinking in this book is informed by the writing and teaching of Maxine Greene. I would like to thank Maxine for continuing to inspire teachers, artists, and children, and for being so generous and dear in reading this manuscript and writing the foreword.

Three educators have been particular mentors to me. Maureen Barbieri introduced me to the work of Maxine Greene, she brought me into staff development, she brought me into NCTE, she brought me to Heinemann, she urged me into the doctoral program at Teachers College, and she propelled me into public education. I look to Maureen's work as the epitome of honesty, intellectual rigor, and generous caring for teachers and children. Maureen is a great gift in my life. Maureen also read and helped me with earlier versions of this manuscript and with the poetry chapter, for which I am thankful.

If Maureen is the reason that I am working in public education, Tom Romano is the reason I am writing. It was in class with Tom Romano that I first wrote a multigenre manuscript, much of which became the inspiration for the work with mythology in Chapter 4. More importantly, Tom made writing a magical endeavor. He helped me find my stride, and he continues to create the conversations about writing that make me want to write and to teach writing.

Shelley Harwayne, presently the superintendent of Community School District Two (soon to be the superintendent of the expanded Region 9), acts as the instructional leader for me in my work as a literacy staff developer. She has believed in this work, she has encouraged me to write about it, and she asks hard questions even as she opens her schools to new ideas. Shelley makes me believe that there will never be circumstances so adverse that we cannot teach in meaningful ways.

There are several schools that opened their doors and their hearts to me and to this work. I am so grateful to the community of P.S./I.S 126, especially Principal Daria Rigney, Assistant Principal Jose Montañez, Karen Lowe (now director at Manhattan Academy of Technology), teachers Teri Foley, Valerie Assantes, Matt

169

Wayne, Renee Houser, Genie Hwang, Heidi Fernandez, and Elisa Sansone, and distinguished teachers Amy Camiri and Dana Caldwell. Every moment in your classrooms is like a jewel in my heart.

I am also grateful to the community of I.S. 89, especially Principal Ellen Foote, teacher and staff developer Donna Santman, and teachers Alex Lee, Gale Treible, Rose Greco (now a mentor teacher at Salk), Jenny Bender, and Audra Kirshbaum. It is with these educators at 89 that I learned what constructive learning experiences look like and what a curriculum of inquiry can mean.

It has been several years since I taught at Marymount School, but it is there that I first found the curricular freedom and the encouragement from colleagues to engage students with the visual arts and with art history. Thank you to Headmistress Sister Kathleen Fagan, Head of the Upper School Carole France, and to fellow teachers Sister Clevie Youngblood, William Davies, John Longo, Martha Erskine, and Barbara Ledig-Sheehan. Marymount supports the arts in schooling in beautiful ways.

To my colleagues and friends, especially staff developers Vicki Vinton, and Debora St. Claire, fellow doctoral students Kiran Purohit and Stacey Fell-Eisenkraft, and my doctoral advisor, Professor Nancy Lesko, thank you for all of the conversations, for the times you read parts of this and related manuscripts, and for the many ways you have taught me about teaching and schooling, some of which appear in this text.

One of the most difficult parts of getting the book to press was assembling the images and arranging copyrights and getting it to look visually the way I hoped it could. Thank you to Eileen Sullivan and Julie Zeftel at the Photograph Library of the Metropolitan Museum of Art, Maria Fernanda Meza of the Artists Rights Society, and Andrea Begel, Timothy McCarthy, and Elizabeth Safford of Art Resource in particular. Thank you to my dear husband, Andy, for faxing and calling museums and photographic agencies all around the world. Thank you also to Evan Reade for designing book covers too beautiful to use. At Heinemann, particular thanks to Eric Chalek and Lynne Reed for their expertise in bringing the manuscript to print.

I would not have begun this book if Bill Varner, then an editor at Heinemann and now one at Stenhouse, hadn't believed in it and helped me get started.

The footprints of Kate Montgomery run throughout this text. I have not worked with an editor before, so I don't know if all editors challenge, support, and redirect. I don't know if all editors read all related texts. But Kate does. She is a scholar and a friend and a writing teacher. I wrote much of the text as a conversation with Kate, and then she showed me ways to make it better.

I wrote this book while working and going to graduate school. And as Jack grew from an infant to a toddler. It never would have been possible if my husband, Andy, and my mother, Kay, had not, each of them, helped me create time to write. Thank you so much. Not just for the time but for the love. Dad, you are not here now to read the final text or Maxine's words, but you are with me in my heart, everyday, in all my endeavors.

Andy, each day you put art into the world and joy in my life. How much I depend on you as a partner and collaborator. Surely I have been lucky to love and be loved by such an artist.

Index